JOURNAL FOR THE STUDY OF THE NEW TESTAMENT SUPPLEMENT SERIES

28

Executive Editor, Supplement Series
David Hill

Publishing Editor
David E Orton

JSOT Press
Sheffield

THE
NOBLE
DEATH

Graeco-Roman Martyrology and Paul's Concept of Salvation

David Seeley

Journal for the Study of the New Testament
Supplement Series 28

To the Macks
for much help and hospitality

Published by JSOT Press
JSOT Press is an imprint of
Sheffield Academic Press Ltd
The University of Sheffield
343 Fulwood Road
Sheffield S10 3BP
England

Printed in Great Britain
by Billing & Sons Ltd
Worcester

British Library Cataloguing in Publication Data

Seeley, David
    The noble death: Graeco-Roman martyrology
    and Paul's concept of salvation.
    1. Bible. N.T.Epistles of Paul. Special subjects: Death
    I. Title   II. Series
    236' .1

    ISSN 0143-5108
    ISBN 1-85075-185-4

CONTENTS

PREFACE

This work originated as a Claremont Graduate School dissertation (1987). To appear in its present form, it has undergone certain revisions, consisting mostly of a drastic reduction in the volume of notes and the near elimination of foreign languages. I have tried my best to ensure that what is thereby gained in convenience and accessibility is not offset by any loss of scholarly integrity.

This work, like any such endeavor, has taken a long time to produce. During that period, I have received help from many people. I am happy for this opportunity to thank them. My advisor, Burton Mack, is included in the dedication (along with B.J. and Burt, Jr). I have benefitted from various discussions with Robert J. Miller (Midway College), Jim Butts (Le Moyne College), Ron Cameron (Wesleyan University), and Richard Smith (The Institute for Antiquity and Christianity). Ernestine Seeley and Jim and Jane Butts were most gracious while I was at Claremont. I have received important assistance from The Institute for Antiquity and Christianity, and from the Religious Studies Department at the University of Montana. My committee members in addition to Dr Mack, J.M. Robinson (Claremont Graduate School), Ron Hock (University of Southern California), and Charles Young (Claremont Graduate School), deserve recognition for the thought they gave to my work. Sandy Summers was invaluable in beginning this project; Dr Ann Heidt was invaluable in bringing it to completion.

Professor David Hill has been a kind and insightful editor.

Debbie DeGolyer and Verna Brown provided admirably efficient typing. The bibliography was prepared by Terri Smith.

Translations from the Bible are according to the Revised Standard Version; translations from 2 and 4 Maccabees are according to the *Oxford Annotated Bible with the Apocrypha,* expanded edition; translations from the German are my own unless otherwise noted.

The fact that this study departs from the beaten track of Pauline scholarship has made its formulation and execution a challenge. However, if I have helped even a little in advancing comprehension of such a seminal figure in our culture as Paul, then my work will have been amply rewarded.

University of Montana
Missoula, Montana
August, 1987

ABBREVIATIONS

AThANT	Abhandlungen zur Theologie des Alten und Neuen Testaments
AOAT	Alter Orient und Altes Testament
AnBib	Analecta Biblica
AB	Anchor Bible
ACW	Ancient Christian Writers
ARW	Archiv für Religionswissenschaft
AVTRW	Aufsätze und Vorträge zur Theologie und Religionswissenschaft
ANRW	*Aufstieg und Niedergang der Römischen Welt*
BFChTh	Beiträge zur Förderung christlicher Theologie
BTS	Biblisch-theologische Studien
BS	Biblische Studien
CBQ	*Catholic Biblical Quarterly*
EPRO	Etudes préliminares aux religions orientales dans l'empire romain
ETL	*Ephemerides Theologicae Lovanienses*
EvO	*Evangelical Quarterly*
EKK	Evangelisch-katholischer Kommentar zum Neuen Testament
ExpT	*Expository Times*
FBESAWK	Forschungen und Berichte der Evangelischen Studiengemeinschaft im Auftrage des Wissenschaftlichen Kuratoriums
FRLANT	Forschungen zur Religion und Literatur des Alten und Neuen Testaments
GTA	Göttingen Theologische Arbeiten
GRBS	Greek, Roman, and Byzantine Studies
HNT	Handbuch zum Neuen Testament
HNTC	Harper's New Testament Commentaries

HDR	Harvard Dissertations in Religion
HTR	*Harvard Theological Review*
HUCA	*Hebrew Union College Annual*
HThK	Herders Theologischer Kommentar zum Neuen Testament
ICC	International Critical Commentary
Int	*Interpretation*
JSNTSS	Journal for the Study of the New Testament Supplement Series
JBL	*Journal of Biblical Literature*
JHS	*Journal of Hellenic Studies*
JJS	*Journal of Jewish Studies*
JTS	*Journal of Theological Studies*
KEK	Kritisch-exegetischer Kommentar über das Neue Testament
LCL	Loeb Classical Library
LL	Lutterworth Library
MNTC	Moffat New Testament Commentary
NEcB	Die Neue Echter Bibel
NTD	Das Neue Testament Deutsch
NA	Neutestamentliche Abhandlungen
NIGTC	The New International Greek Testament Commentary
NTS	New Testament Studies
NTTS	New Testament Tools and Studies
NovT	*Novum Testamentum*
OBO	Orbis Biblicus et Orientalis
PTS	Paderborner Theologische Studien
QD	*Quaestiones Disputatae*
RNS	Regensburger Neues Testament
RR	*Religion and Reason*
RVV	Religionsgeschichtliche Versuche und Vorarbeiten
RB	*Revue Biblique*
SCS	Sather Classical Studies
SBG	Schweizerisches Bibelwerk für die Gemeinde
SJT	*Scottish Journal of Theology*
SBLDS	Society of Biblical Literature Dissertation Series
SWJT	*Southwest Journal of Theology*
SVTP	Studia in Verteris Testamenti Pseudepigrapha

SPB	Studia Post-Biblica
StANT	Studien zum Alten und Neuen Testament
SUNT	Studien zur Umwelt des Neuen Testaments
SBT	Studies in Biblical Theology
SCA	Studies in Christian Antiquity
SNTSMS	Studiorum Novi Testamenti Societas Monograph Series
SBS	Stuttgarter Bibelstudien
SNT	Supplements to Novum Testamentum
TDNT	*Theological Dictionary of the New Testament*
TS	Theological Studies
ThHK	Theologischer Handkommentar zum Neuen Testament
TLZ	*Theologische Literaturzeitung*
TR	*Theologische Rundschau*
ThS	Theologische Studien
TZ	*Theologische Zeitschrift*
WMANT	Wissenschaftliche Monographien zum Alten und Neuen Testament
ZNW	*Zeitschrift für die neutestamentliche Wissenschaft*
ZTK	*Zeitschrift für Theologie und Kirche*

INTRODUCTION

This study begins with the question, 'What historical influences have shaped Paul's interpretation of Jesus' death?' Chapter 1 discusses Paul's references to the Temple cultus. Chapter 2 treats his use of the Suffering Servant from Isaiah 53. Chapter 3 deals with the appearance of the Binding of Isaac (Genesis 22) in the Pauline corpus. Chapter 4 examines the influence of Mystery religions on Paul. Through close exegesis, the conclusion is reached that the items studied by these chapters have not had a formative impact on Paul's soteriology. Chapter 5, however, finds striking similarities between the martyrs' deaths in *4 Maccabees* (written 20–54 CE) and Jesus' death in Paul. This chapter isolates a cluster of five components shared by *4 Maccabees'* interpretation of the martyrs' deaths and by Paul's interpretation of Jesus' death. This cluster is termed the Noble Death. Chapter 6 pursues this concept into its original context, namely, Hellenistic and Roman philosophy.

The five components of the Noble Death are as follows: (1) obedience, (2) the overcoming of physical vulnerability, (3) a military setting, (4) vicariousness, or the quality of being beneficial for others, and (5) sacrificial metaphors.

Chapter 5 shows that these five components are readily apparent in *4 Maccabees*. The martyrs remain obedient to the law by overcoming their physical vulnerability and enduring tortuous deaths. A military cast is given to the situation by the Maccabean revolt and by the fact that the martyrs are locked in a sort of combat with their persecutor. If the martyrs disobey, then they lose; if they remain obedient, then they win. Needless to say, they win. One of the martyrs cries that they have 'paralyzed' their opponent's power and shown its ultimate impotence (12.24-27). The martyrs are admired for their obedience (18.3), their example revives observance of the law throughout Israel (18.4), and their persecutor, unable to make anyone else break the law, gives up and leaves (18.5). This indicates that the vicarious benefit of the martyrs' deaths is imparted mimetically. Others imitate or re-enact the martyrs' death-defying obedience in their own lives. Thereby, they become freed from the power of the evil tyrant (cf. also 1.11).

The author of *4 Maccabees* hopes that his audience will be likewise inspired by the martyrs' examples. He meticulously details the deaths so that his readers will re-enact them imaginatively (cf. e.g. 14.9-10). Having mentally experienced the worst and having seen that obedience can still be maintained, the readers will be more capable of exercising such discipline in their own lives. They will thus benefit.

At 6.28-29 and 17.21-22, sacrificial metaphors are applied to the martyrs' deaths. But exegesis reveals that these passages are consciously metaphorical treatments of the more basic, mimetic pattern.

After dealing with *4 Maccabees*, Chapter 5 proceeds to locate the same five elements in Paul.

The importance of obedience for Paul's understanding of Jesus' death is demonstrated through close scrutiny of Phil. 2.8 and Rom. 5.19. The notion of overcoming physical vulnerability is raised in Romans 7, where Paul addresses the effect of Sin. (I capitalize the word here because of the personified aspect it takes on in Paul's thought.) In Romans 7, Paul states that Sin, operating through flesh, counters the inner man's desire to obey God's law. Interpreting this anthropological assertion christologically, one realizes that Jesus, too, would have been subject to such compulsion. Yet, he overcame his physical vulnerability as a human and was obedient even to death (cf. also 2 Cor. 5.21). This obedient death broke the power of the old aeon ruled by Sin and Death (Rom. 6.10). It established another aeon, ruled by Christ and locked in virtual military combat with the old aeon (Rom. 6.16-22, 1 Thess. 5.8).

The means by which the vicarious benefit of Jesus' death is imparted to Christians is surprisingly close to the manner in which such benefit is imparted by the Maccabeean martyrs. In each case, the crucial factor is re-enactment. In *4 Mac-*

cabees, the martyrs' fellow-citizens or the treatise's readers imaginatively re-enact the deaths and are thus strengthened for facing a literal re-enactment. In Romans 6, a re-enactment is still very much at issue, but the literal and the imaginative are curiously mixed in the baptismal rite. Paul cannot mean that people cease functioning biologically when they re-enact Jesus' death; yet, he must intend more than a simple, imaginative recapitulation. Paul seems to believe that, when people re-enact Jesus' death, they, too, share the effects of its obedience and are henceforth released from Sin's compelling power. They do not literally have to die an obedient death; however, the ritual re-enactment is for Paul nonetheless an objective and definitive element.

Chapter 5 takes note of the sacrificial metaphors which Paul attaches to Jesus' death, but it refers the reader back to Chapter 1, where extensive exegesis demonstrates the ancillary nature of such metaphors.

In Chapter 6, the study proceeds to the original context of the five elements known together as the Noble Death. This context is Hellenistic and Roman philosophy.

For instance, the philosopher Epictetus (c. 50–c. 120 CE) asserts that Diogenes the Cynic would allow no one to be more obedient to divine commands than he. He was always prepared to overcome his physical vulnerability by simply giving up his 'whole paltry body' for the sake of this obedience (4.1.152-55). Seneca (c. 4 BCE–65 CE) praises a series of men who suffer and die in obedience to what they believe is right (*Epistle* 24). Their obedience is maintained in the face of horrible assaults on their physical vulnerability.

A military setting for the philosopher's Noble Death becomes evident when Epictetus paraphrases Socrates' defense speech before the court in Athens. The philosopher, says Socrates, is like a good soldier. He has been stationed by God at a particular post, and should hold it even at the cost of his life (*Ep.* 1.9.24). Similarly, Seneca shows his model philosopher, Cato the Elder, locked in combat with Fortuna, and nullifying all her attacks on him by the integrity of his death (*Ep.* 24.7).

As for vicariousness, once again the heart of the matter is re-enactment. Seneca summons up various exemplary martyrs who benefit others by showing that one can successfully endure all the tortures to which fortune may subject a person (*Ep.* 24.9). By imaginatively re-enacting the martyr's suffering and death, one gains courage to follow what is right and resists all compulsion to the contrary. In this vein, Seneca says that Socrates bravely remained in prison 'in order to free mankind from the fear of two most grievous things, death and imprisonment' (*Ep.* 24.4). By mentally re-enacting this example, a person becomes liberated from the compelling force by which death influences behaviour, namely, fear. In a sense, one is released from death's power. Seneca neatly sums up this whole process when he asks why good men suffer. His answer: 'It is that they may teach others to endure ... they were born to be a pattern (*in exemplar*)' (*De Prov.* 6.2-3).

Occasionally, the philosopher's death is metaphorized as a sacrifice. This takes place in Lucan (*Pharsalia* 2.304-18), Tacitus (*Annals* 15.94; 16.35), and Lucian ('Demonax' 11). As with *4 Maccabees* and Paul, such metaphors are secondary to the more basic, mimetic model.

This investigation thus reveals a very strong family resemblance between *4 Maccabees*, Paul, and Greco-Roman philsophers. There is not presently available the data which would allow one to pin down exactly how and where Paul came into contact with the Noble Death. It is suggestive, however that when Seneca lists his exemplary martyrs, he anticipates the objection that their deeds have been 'droned to death in all the schools' (*Ep.* 24.6). Paul knew Hebrew, but he wrote in Greek. He was a student at Jerusalem, but he was born in the Hellenistic city of Tarsus. It is not difficult to surmise that he went to school and studied Greek at some point in his life.[1] In school, he may well have encountered the Noble Death. Another possibility is that this concept was so tightly woven into the fabric of Hellenistic culture that Paul assimilated it without even trying. In any case, the examination shows Paul to have been a man of his time, and exhibits a fun-

---

1 Cf. C. Forbes, 'Comparison, Self-Praise and Irony: Paul's Boasting and the Conventions of Hellenistic Rhetoric', *NTS* 32 (1986) 1-30.

damental continuity between his thought and that of his contemporaries.[1]

---

1 The discussion in Chapter 6 is based largely on Seneca, Epictetus, Dio Chrysos-
tom, Plutarch, and the historian Silius Italicus. (However, cf. also Cicero, *Tusc.*
2.21.49–2.23.54.) Objections to this group can be raised on the ground of chrono-
logy, and so the issue should be addressed briefly here. Epictetus, Dio, and
Plutarch were born sometime around the middle of the first century CE. Silius was
born in 26 CE. However, Seneca, who amply attests to the Noble Death, was born in
four BCE, thus making him an exact contemporary of Jesus and Paul. The overall
trdition within which Seneca and the others work seems stable during this period.
No sudden rupture, such as occurred in Judaism at 70 CE, disturbed its continuity.
There is thus no particular reason to imagine serious distinctions between, say,
Epictetus and his teacher, Musonius Rufus. The former's references to the latter
uniformly place him in a positive, authoritative light (1.1.27; 1.7.32; 1.9.29-
30;3.6.10; 3.15.14; 3.23.29). Indeed, the first of these references cites Musonius as
an authority in a section clearly devoted to the sort of death with which we are concerned. Unfortunately, the thought of Musonius and, doubtless, many other Cynic
and Stoic philosophers prior to the first century CE has survived only in fragments
or not at all.

Chapter 1

PAUL'S DOCTRINE OF SALVATION
AND THE TEMPLE CULTUS

Introduction

In this chapter, we will determine how likely it is that the Temple cultus had a formative influence on Paul's soteriology.[1] This determination is necessary because it is often asserted that Paul understood Jesus' death in terms of the sacrificial activity which went on at the temple in Jerusalem. This chapter will proceed step by step, looking in turn at each of the passages that scholars have described as possessing cultic elements. We will, of course, try to decide whether the passages themselves exhibit these elements, but of even greater importance will be the extent to which Paul integrates such elements into the wider context of his thinking about Jesus' death. Isolated allusions to the Temple cultus would be one thing; a systematic employment of the Temple to interpret Jesus' death would be something else.

Romans 3.25

This verse, thought by many to be from a pre-Pauline tradition,[2] contains the word *hilasterion*. The latter may refer to the

---

[1] Among those who assert the importance of cultic categories for Paul are: H. Gese, *Zur biblischen Theologie* (Munich: Kaiser, 1977) 105; O. Kuss, 'Die theologischen Grundgedanken des Hebräerbriefes. Zur Deutung des Todes Jesu im Neuen Testament'. *Auslegung und Verkündigung* (3 vols; Regensburg: Pustet, 1963) 1.291. Others, however, downplay the role of cultic categories in Paul: J.C. Beker, *Paul the Apostle* (Philadelphia: Fortress, 1980) 197; R. Bultmann, *Theology of the New Testament* (trans. K. Grobel; 2 vols; New York: Scribner, 1951) 1.297-98; E.P. Sanders, *Paul and Palestinian Judaism* (Philadelphia: Fortress, 1977) 499.

[2] Rudolf Bultmann indicated the possibility in 'Neueste Paulusforschung', *TR* 8 (1936) 11-12; he presented 3.25 as traditional in *Theology* 1.46. Ernst Käsemann developed this position in 'Zum Verständnis von Römer 3, 24-26', *ZNW* 43 (1050-

mercy-seat, or cover of the Ark of the Covenant. It was on this cover that blood was sprinkled during the Day of Atonement. If *hilasterion* does refer to the mercy-seat, then it would, despite its possible pre-Pauline origins, constitute important evidence for cultic influence on Paul's thought. Those who take it thus are numerous,[1] but so are those who do not.[2] The former insist on two major points, the first more specific, and the second more general: (1) in the Septuagint, *hilasterion* is a technical term for the mercy-seat; (2) there is an evident appropriateness to elucidating Jesus' death through that Temple ritual which dealt most comprehensively with sin, namely, the Day of Atonement. An ancillary point is that the mention of blood supports a cultic framework.

Those who disagree with this interpretation do so chiefly because of six points: (1) *hilasterion* in 3.25 does not have the definite article, while it does in the Septuagint;[3] (2) the verse's context offers little or nothing that points to a cultic frame of reference; (3) if Jesus were to be regarded as the mercy-seat, he would then have to be sprinkled with his own blood, a most awkward image; (4) the mercy-seat was hidden, but this *hilasterion* has been set forth openly; (5) the comparison would be lost on Paul's Gentile readers, who were unfamiliar with the Temple apparatus; (6) Paul does not elaborate or even use this particular language anywhere else.

---

51) 150-54. It has since been widely accepted. There are those, however, who continue to maintain that Rom. 3.25 is Pauline, e.g.: C.K. Barrett, *A Commentary on the Epistle to the Romans* (New York: Harper, 1957) 74-82; F.F. Bruce, *The Epistle of Paul to the Romans* (Grand Rapids: Eerdmans, 1963) 102-108.

1 Among the many authors who assert that *hilasterion* refers to the mercy-seat are the following: E. Brunner, *Der Römerbrief* (Kassel: Oncken, 1938) 23; Bruce, *Romans* 106; T.W. Manson, 'Romans', *Peake's Commentary* (ed. M. Black; New York: Thomas Nelson, 1962) 943; P. Stuhlmacher, 'Zur neueren Exegese von Röm 3.24-26', *Jesus und Paulus* (eds. E.E. Ellis & E. Grässer; Göttingen: Vandenhoeck & Ruprecht, 1975) 321-32.

2 The following are among the many who either deny that *hilasterion* signifies the mercy-seat, or specify expiation or propitiation as its meaning: C.E.B. Cranfield, *A Critical and Exegetical Commentary on the The Epistle to the Romans* (ICC, 82; 2 vols; Edinburgh: T. & T. Clark, 1975-77) 1.214-15; D. Hill, *Greek Words and Hebrew Meanings: Studies in the Semantics of Soteriological Terms* (SNTSMS, 5; Cambridge: Cambridge University Press, 1967) 43; L. Morris, 'The Meaning of ἱλαστήριον in Romans iii.25', *NTS* 2 (1955) 34-42; E.P. Sanders, *Paul and Palestinian Judaism* 466-67.

3 The single exception is Ex. 25.17, where, however, *epithema* has been added for identification.

The debate between these two sides continues. For instance, Stuhlmacher has argued that, according to the ninth edition of Blass–Debrunner's Greek grammar, the article is normally absent with a predicate nominative.[1] But Friedrich retorts that, according to the fourteenth edition, the article is absent if the predicate nominative designates an abstract quality attributed to an item.[2] The article is present, however, if the predicate nominative refers to the item itself.[3] Were *hilasterion* to refer specifically to the mercy-seat, therefore, it would require the article.

The question of context has also been disputed. Again Stuhlmacher must be considered, for he has been the most notable recent commentator to insist that the context of 3.25 supports a reference to the Day of Atonement.[4] Rom. 3.23-25, he says, contains a creation motif which echoes Lev. 16.9. The occurrence of 'glory' in v. 23 refers to Adam's original glory which he lost in the Fall.[5] It is difficult to see, however, that Paul is actually engaging in such speculation at this point, or that it would necessarily connect with the cultic celebration of the Day of Atonement if he were.

It is also hard to understand why Stuhlmacher believes that the theme of remission of sin, as a demonstration of God's forbearance and righteousness, connects Rom. 3.23-25 with the Day of Atonement. The latter does provide remission of sins, but says nothing about God's patience or forbearance.[6] Nor does the Day Atonement seem to address specifically the issue of forgiveness as a demonstration of God's righteousness. Indeed, Sam Williams has explained the background of 3.25b without any reference to the Temple cultus at all.[7]

---

1 Stuhlmacher, 'Zur neueren Exegese' 322-23.
2 G. Friedrich, *Die Verkündigung des Todes Jesu im Neuen Testament* (BTS, 6; Neukirchen-Vluyn: Neukirchener Verlag, 1982) 62.
3 F. Blass, A. Debrunner, and F. Rehkopf, *Grammatik des neutestamentlichen Griechisch* (14th edn; Göttingen: Vandenhoeck & Ruprecht, 1976) Section 273.
4 P. Stuhlmacher, 'Theologische Probleme gegenwärtiger Paulusinterpretation', *TLZ* 98 (1973) 727; cf. also 'Zur neueren Exegese' 322.
5 Stuhlmacher, 'Theologische Probleme', 732n17; cf. also 'Zur neueren Exegese' 322n64.
6 In a later formulation of this point, Stuhlmacher has omitted any specific reference to God's patience or forebearance ('Zur neueren Exegese' 322).
7 S.K. Williams, *Jesus' Death as Saving Event: The Origin of a Concept* (HDR 2; Missoula, Montana: Scholars, 1975) 52; cf. also 19-34.

Manson has asserted that the 'long indictment of Gentiles and Jews in chs. i–iii is really an elaborate confession of sin for all mankind', and that this corresponds to the High Priest's confession on the Day of Atonement.[1] Morris, however, retorts that chs. 1–3 are really intended to show all humankind fallen under the sway of sin, 'whether they acknowledge it or not'.[2]

Gifford argues that 'redemption' (*apolutrosis*) in 3.24 injects the concept of atonement, and that mention of the law in v. 21 sets the stage for the mercy-seat, 'the very centre and core' of the Law.[3] But both connections are forced. Redemption and atonement are not necessarily related, and it is doubtful that mere mention of the Law would put anyone in mind of the mercy-seat in particular.

Stuhlmacher lists the reference to blood as part of 3.25's cultic tone, but here, too, reservations must be expressed.[4] Several authors have pointed out that the reference to Jesus' blood can mean simply his violent death.[5] Fitzer believes the phrase should be interpreted in terms of the violent fates of the prophets (cf. Matt. 23.30, 35; Luke 11.50; Rev. 16.16, 17.6, 18.24) or the martyrs (Rev. 6.10, 19.2).[6] This accords with Williams' position that the phrase represents a little-used 'instrumental dative of price'[7] and should be rendered 'at the cost/price of his blood'.[8]

1 T.W. Manson, ʹΙΛΑΣΤΗΡΙΟΝʹ *JTS* 46 (1945) 7.
2 L. Morris, *The Apostolic Preaching of the Cross* (3rd edn; Grand Rapids: Eerdmans, 1965) 192.
3 E.H. Gifford, *The Epistle of St. Paul to the Romans* (London: John Murray, 1886) 97; on context cf. also A. Nygren, *Commentary on Romans* (Philadelphia: Muhlenburg, 1949) 157-59.
4 This remains, however, a common stance; among those who take it are Bruce, *Romans* 107; C.H. Dodd, *The Epistle of Paul to the Romans* (Moffat New Testament Commentary, 6; New York: Harper, 1932) 55-56 (Dodd nevertheless proceeds to exegete this reference in a distinctly martyrological direction); U. Wilckens, *Der Brief an die Römer* (EKK, 6; 3 parts; Zürich: Benziger Verlag; Neukirchen-Vluyn: Neukirchener Verlag, 1978-82) 1.190.
5 B. Weiss, *Kritisch-exegetisches Handbuch über den Brief des Paulus an die Römer* (7th edn; Göttingen: Vandenhoeck & Ruprecht, 1886) 180n**.
6 G. Fitzer, 'Der Ort der Versöhnung nach Paulus', *TZ* 22 (1966) 173.
7 N. Turner, *Syntax* (Edinburgh: T. & T. Clark, 1963) 253; vol. 3 of J.H. Moulton, *A Grammar of the Greek New Testament* (3 vols; Edinburgh: T. & T. Clark, 1906-63).
8 Williams, *Jesus' Death* 46-47.

In any case, considering 'blood' to be a sign of cultic thought still leaves problems. As mentioned, Jesus must then be sprinkled with his own blood. Adherents of the cultic view assert that Heb. 9.11-14 (where Jesus is both high priest and sacrifice) shows that such a conception was possible.[1] But Morris[2] and Cranfield[3] have both objected that Rom. 3.25, taken thus, would be even more convoluted than Heb. 9.11-14.

We come now to the issue of the hidden mercy-seat and the openly set forth *hilasterion*. This is perhaps the most paradoxical of the points listed above, since both camps claim it for support. Those against the equation of *hilasterion* and the mercy-seat believe it introduces an unwieldy contradiction into the supposed simile. But for those who advocate the equation, it signals a clear, antitypical structure. Indeed, Schmidt claims that it is the strongest argument for regarding *hilasterion* as the mercy-seat.[4] But Morris reminds us that, for such an antitypical figure to work, the relation between *hilasterion* and the mercy-seat would have to be immediately and clearly understood.[5] That Paul's readers were sufficiently informed for this, however, is not at all evident.

Stuhlmacher points to 1 Peter, 1 Clement, and the Shepherd of Hermas as proof that the Roman church would indeed have understood such a connection.[6] Lyonnet[7] points simply to the epistle itself as proof, and Büchsel[8] points to Paul's epistles in general. Wilckens simply mentions the centrality of Lev. 16 in Hebrew tradition as the determining factor.[9]

However, powerful voices have been raised in opposition to this stance.[10] The basic problem, of course, is that we know so little about the Roman church. But Paul's concern throughout

---

1 Stuhlmacher, 'Theologische Probleme' 728; Wilckens, *Römer* 1.191-92.

2 Morris, *Apostolic Preaching* 195-96.

3 Cranfield, *Romans* 1.215.

4 H.W. Schmidt, *Der Brief des Paulus an die Römer* (ThHK 6; Berlin: Evangelische Verlagsanstalt, 1962) 68.

5 Morris, *Apostolic Preaching* 197.

6 Stuhlmacher, 'Zur neueren Exegese', 322; cf. also 'Theologische Probleme', 727-28.

7 S. Lyonnet and L. Sabourin, *Sin, Redemption, and Sacrifice* (AnBib, 48; Rome: Biblical Institute, 1970) 163-64.

8 F. Büchsel, 'ἱλαστήριον', *TDNT* 3.323.

9 Wilckens, *Römer* 1.191.

10 Friedrich, *Verkündigung* 64.

Romans over the status of Gentiles, plus specific references
like 1.13 and 11.13-31, show that his readers belonged to a
predominantly Hellenistic-Christian church.[1] Would it be
reasonable to expect a 'grafted shoot' (11.17) to sense immediately such a tricky figure of speech? Wouldn't Paul have
added at least some marker to make sure his readers got the
point and to prevent them from feeling inferior to more
knowledgeable Jewish-Christians? It would seem so.

Finally, there is the issue of the uniqueness of 3.25 within the
Pauline corpus. Not only does Paul fail to elaborate any comparison of Jesus and the mercy-seat here, he never even
mentions it anywhere else. There is the possibility that Paul
did so in some letter now lost to us, but it remains curious that
such an intriguing and pregnant figure would not appear
again in what we have.[2]

It appears, therefore, that the comparison of *hilasterion* and
the mercy-seat at Rom. 3.25 is unlikely. The lack of supporting context, the absence of an article, the general awkwardness of the imagery, Paul's Gentile readership, and the
uniqueness of the language in Paul's letters all count against
seeing this verse as an indication that Jesus is the cover of that
Ark.

What, then, is the meaning of *hilasterion*? Morris,[3] Hill,[4]
and Williams[5] have answered this question with the aid of *4
Maccabees*, which Williams rightly calls 'the closest available
non-Christian parallel'.[6] Written during Paul's lifetime,[7]
4 Maccabees 17.22 says that God delivered Israel through the

---

1 H.-J. van der Minde, *Schrift und Tradition bei Paulus* (PTS 3; Munich, Paderborn, and Vienna: Schöningh, 1976) 194; cf. the literature cited on 194n20.
2 Cf. F. Godet, *Commentary on St. Paul's Epistle to the Romans* (trans. A. Cusin;
   ed. T.W. Chambers; 2nd edn of translation; New York: Funk & Wagnalls, 1883)
   151.
3 Morris, *Apostolic Reading* 159, 195, 197-98.
4 Hill, *Greek Words* 41-47.
5 Williams, *Jesus' Death* 40-41.
6 Williams, *Jesus' Death* 40.
7 E. Bickermann, 'The Date of Fourth Maccabees', *Louis Ginzberg Jubilee Volume*
   (New York: The American Academy for Jewish Research, 1945) 105-12; J.A.
   Goldstein, *II Maccabees* (AB, 1a; Garden City, New York: Doubleday, 1983) 26; M.
   Hadas, *The Third and Fourth Books of Maccabees* (New York: Harper, 1953) 95-
   99; Hill, *Greek Words* 43; E. Lohse, *Märtyrer und Gottesknecht* (Göttingen: Vandenhoeck & Ruprecht, 1955) 69n2; Williams, *Jesus' Death* 197-202.

hilasterion of the death of the martyrs.[1] Wilckens maintains that this phrase constitutes cultic, technical language, but his reason is only that the Jewish author must have meant it thus.[2] It is more likely that the general sense of a simple 'propitiatory' or 'expiatory' death is intended here.[3] Which of these two terms better suits the *hilaskesthai* family of words has long been debated.[4] However, Williams points out that both meanings are present in *4 Maccabees*. Phrases such as 'to purify' (1.11, 17.21) and 'purification' (6.29) show that the removal of sin and its effects, i.e., expiation, is in view. But 4.21 makes plain that God's wrath has become a factor in the situation, as well. Indeed, it is just this wrath which sets Antiochus Epiphanes against the Jews, and which thus brings about the martyrs' suffering.[5] Hence, one can say that the martyrs' deaths constitute an expiation which propitiates God's wrath in so far as it removes the latter's cause. The same may plausibly be said of Rom. 3.25. Paul often indicates that the sin to which believers were subject has now been done away with (e.g., Rom. 5.8-9; 8.3; 1 Cor. 5.7). At the same time, the early chapters of Romans stress that all humankind, both Jew and Gentile, lies under God's wrath (1.18; 3.5). Thus, even if expiation is perhaps a better single-word translation for *hilasterion*, the thought of propitiation should not be excluded.

We have seen that *hilasterion* in Rom. 3.25 is probably not to be linked with the mercy-seat of the Temple, but instead should be taken to mean a propitiating expiation. Now that

---

1 On the textual problems of this verse, cf. N. Brox, *Zeuge und Märtyrer* (StANT 5; Munich: Kösel, 1961) 150-51; Williams, *Jesus' Death* 40-41n87.

2 Wilckens, *Römer* 1.192n538.

3 In *4 Maccabees* 17.22, *hilasterion* is parallel to the non-cultic term *antipsuchon*. Verse 21 does refer to purification of the land, but no cultic connotation is evident. Indeed, the verse is set within a chapter marked by philosophical, athletic, and military metaphors (n.b. 17.11-16). Added to these considerations is *4 Maccabees'* strongly Hellenistic flavor. It is, for instance, written in sophisticated Greek, cf. U. Breitenstein, *Beobachtungen zu Sprache, Stil und Gedankengut des Vierten Makkabäerbuchs* (Basel and Stutgart: Schwabe, 1976) chs. 1–3 *passim*. It is also strongly influenced by Hellenistic philosophy, cf. R. Renehan, 'The Greek Philosophic Background of Fourth Maccabees', *Rheinisches Museum für Philologie* 115 (1972) 222-38.

4 Cf. *inter alia* Morris, *Apostolic Reading* 144-213; N.H. Young, '"Hilaskesthai" and Related Words in the New Testament' *EvQ* 55 (1983) 169-70.

5 Williams, *Jesus' Death* 41.

this has been determined, let us move on to a closer analysis of how 3.25 functions in its context.

Paul uses 3.25 to make the point that, in Jesus, God has manifested his righteousness in a new way. This way is new because it is 'apart from law' (3.21a)[1] and instead operates 'through faith' (3.22). Should we then reconsider the possibility that Paul is using 3.25 to formulate an antitypical contrast between Jesus (the new, faith-oriented *hilasterion*) and the Law (as represented by the old mercy-seat)? No. Paul's use of Law in this section of Romans is more complex and more characteristic of his own peculiar stance than such an antitype would suggest. As noted, 3.21a rejects the Law. But 3.21b says that the Law nevertheless bears witness to the new way of manifesting God's righteousness. Paul thus both denies and affirms the Law. The same thought is echoed in verses 28 and 31. The former states that justification comes by faith 'apart from works of law'. But the latter says that faith upholds the Law! This double-edged approach makes sense only in light of Paul's later elucidation of Law and Sin. In chs. 5–7, Sin is shown to be more than just individual transgression; rather, it is a kind of cosmic power holding people under its sway and working through the Law and flesh. In Rom. 7.10, Paul phrases the paradox succinctly: 'the very commandment which promised life proved to be death to me'. Sin is not breaking the law, it is following the Law in a way which begins in moral responsibility, but which Sin as a power inevitably bends towards self-aggrandizement. This is the 'boasting' of 3.27.[2] So, even if 3.25 were suggesting an antitypical contrast between law and faith (which the above analysis of *hilasterion* shows to be unlikely), there would still be a sizeable gap between that pattern and Paul's own theology. The type/antitype pattern is much simpler than Paul's own, simultaneous affirmation and denial of the Law. The somewhat confusing qualification Paul makes at 5.13 is an example of how much more complicated his own position was. This

---

1 On how Paul's use of 'the law and the prophets' in 3.21 relates to his use of 'the law' alone in 3.31, and on how both verses relate to Rom. 4, cf. P. von der Osten-Sacken, *Römer 8 als Beispiel paulinischer Soteriologie* (Göttingen: Vandenhoeck & Ruprecht, 1975) 245-50.
2 Beker, *Paul the Apostle* 80-83.

complication is, of course, caused by his non-cultic conception of Sin as a cosmic power.

To summarize: (1) *hilasterion* probably means not mercy-seat, but propitiating expiation, as it does in *4 Maccabees* 17.22; (2) even if *hilasterion* were to mean mercy-seat, it would still be true that Paul has not developed any such cultic simile in the context; (3) on the contrary, the context reveals the more cosmically directed patterns of thought, of which Paul makes profound use later in Romans. We must conclude, therefore, that the cultus has not had a significant impact on Paul at this point.

Romans 5.9

Like Rom. 3.25, Rom. 5.9 has been called traditional (though by far fewer exegetes).[1] Also like 3.25, its reference to blood has often been taken as possessing a cultic background.[2] However, others have maintained that blood here refers only to Jesus' death, and does not include cultic connotations.[3] On the side of the former is, of course, the word and its frequent appearance in a sacrificial context.[4] But on the side of the latter is the fact that Paul seems to make no use of that context. Indeed, the orientation of Rom. 5 is cosmic rather than sacrificial.[5] The reference of 5.6 to the period when 'we were still weak' signifies human enslavement by the malevolent power of Sin.[6] This is shown by the fact that in 5.8 Paul refers to the same period as 'while we were yet sinners'. Paul can equate weakness and being a sinner because he conceives of Sin as a

---

1 H. Conzelmann, *An Outline of the Theology of the New Testament* (New York and Evanston, Ill.: Harper, 1969) 70; E. Lohse, *Märtyrer* 139.

2 J. Jeremias, *Der Opfertod Jesu Christ* (Calwer Hefte 62; 2nd edn; Stuttgart: Calwer, 1966) 16; R. Daly, *Christian Sacrifice* (SCA 18; Washington, D.C.: The Catholic University of America Press, 1978) 119n74; E. Lohse, *Märtyrer* 138-39; Stuhlmacher, 'Zur neueren Exegese' 324.

3 G. Eichholz, *Die Theologie des Paulus im Umriss* (Neukirchen-Vluyn: Neukirchener Verlag, 1972) 166; H. Schlier, *Der Römerbrief* (HThK, 6; Freiburg, Basel, and Vienna: Herder, 1977) 155.

4 Conzelmann, *Outline* 70; W.D. Davies, *Paul and Rabbinic Judaism* (4th edn; Philadelphia: Fortress, 1980) 236.

5 Beker, *Paul the Apostle* 191.

6 V.P. Furnish, *Theology and Ethics in Paul* (Nashville and New York: Abingdon, 1968) 149; R. Pesch, *Römerbrief* (NEcB 6; Würzburg: Echter Verlag, 1983) 50.

power. Weakness in the face of its compulsion results in one's becoming a sinner. The use of 'enemies' in 5.10 does suggest a sense of responsibility more appropriate to Sin as individual transgressions than as a power. However, 5.12 shows that the conception of Sin as a power remains fundamental. It entered the world through Adam. All men sinned, it is true, and so became 'infected' with it. But they then became slaves to sin, rather than continuing perpetrators of it. (Perhaps the clearest explication of this occurs later, in 7.17, where Paul says that it is no longer he who does the thing he hates, 'but sin which dwells within me'; cf. also Rom. 9.19; 11.32.)

The Adam-Christ typology of 5.12-21 presupposes the conception of Sin as a power. Adam and Christ stand, in Nygren's words, 'as the respective heads of the two aeons'.[1] Those whose lives are conducted within each aeon are unavoidably influenced by its structure. In one, Sin reigns, and in the other, grace (5.21). Rom. 5.9 can readily be fitted into this pattern. The believers have been transferred from the old, Adamic aeon where they lived under the threat of God's wrath (5.9b).[2] This transfer has placed them in a state of reconciliation with God (5.10-11), as though peace had been declared between two warring sides.[3] This suggestion of two warring sides is more akin to Sin as a power opposed to God than to sin as a collection of individual transgressions. Paul does not speak of sins being forgiven or atoned for, but of reconciliation between hostile forces. The reference to God's wrath gives a decidedly apocalyptic tone to the passage, a fact which implies that the aeons so typical of apocalypticisim are indeed at issue here.

Rom. 5.9 and its context seem best explained, therefore, by a conception of Sin that has little to do with the Temple cultus.

---

1 Nygren, *Romans* 210.
2 E. Käsemann, 'The Saving Significance of Jesus' Death in Paul', *Perspectives on Paul* (trans. M. Kohl; Philadelphia: Fortress, 1971) 44.
3 Bultmann, *Theology* 1.286; Nygren, *Romans* 204-205; Schmidt, *Römer* 94.

Romans 8.3

The phrase 'for sin' has often been taken to refer to the cultic sin-offering (*hattat*).[1] The Septuagint employs just this phrase to translate *hattat* at, e.g., Lev. 4.3, 14; 5.6. Nevertheless, many deny such a connection, generally citing the lack of any indication by Paul that this is what he meant.[2] Indeed, the context shows that 'for sin' should be interpreted in aeon or cosmic categories rather than cultic ones.[3] Rom. 8.1 speaks of those who are 'in Christ Jesus', a phrase which Rom. 5 and 6 have explicated as signifying a sphere of power over against the old sphere of Adamic Sin.[4] These two spheres are further characterized in 8.2 as 'the law of the Spirit of life in Christ Jesus' on the one hand, and 'the law of sin and death' on the other. Paul uses 'law' here to signify two contrasting orders of existence, one ruled by Christ and leading to life, the other ruled by sin and leading to death.[5] Paul says nothing here about sin being expiated, but instead uses the language of liberation: the Law of the Spirit has set him free from the Law of Sin and death. This suggests the old law was a prison or tyrant. In verses 4-5, these two orders of existence appear again, now in terms of walking/living according to the flesh or according to the spirit.

Given this context, it is reasonable to conclude that 8.3 involves the same concepts. Christ was sent into the sphere ruled by Sin ('in the likeness of sinful flesh'), died sinlessly (cf.

---

1 Daly, *Christian Sacrifice* 239; J.D.G. Dunn, *Christology in the Making* (Philadelphia: Westminster, 1980) 45; E. Käsemann, *Commentary on Romans* (trans. and ed. G.W. Bromiley; Grand Rapids: Eerdmans, 1980) 216.

2 Dodd, *Romans* 156; Friederich, *Verkündigung* 69-70; E. Lohse, *Märtyrer* 153n6.

3 E. Brandenburger, *Adam und Christus* (WMANT, 7; Neukirchen-Vluyn: Neukirchener Verlag, 1962) 236-37; G. Delling, *Der Kreuzestod Jesu in der urchristlichen Verkündigung* (Göttingen: Vandenhoeck & Ruprecht, 1972) 20; E. Schweizer, 'Dying and Rising with Christ', *NTS* 14 (1967) 13.

4 Cf. *inter alia*, P. Althaus, *Der Brief an die Römer* (NTD 6; 9th edn; Göttingen: Vandenhoeck & Ruprecht, 1959) 79; E. Brandenburger, *Fleisch und Geist* (WMANT, 29; Neukirchen-Vluyn: Neukirchener Verlag, 1968) 56-57.

5 G. Friedrich, 'Das Gesetz des Glaubens Röm. 3.27', *TZ* 10 (1954) 406-407, argues that 'the law of the Spirit of life' denotes the Torah in a literal fashion. Others, however, assert a figurative use of 'law' here: Käsemann, *Romans* 213, 215; O. Kuss, *Der Römerbrief* (3 vols; Regensburg: Pustet, 1963-78) 2.490; O. Michel, *Der Brief an die Römer* (KEK, 4; 5th edn; Göttingen: Vandenhoeck & Ruprecht, 1978) 255-57.

2 Cor. 5.21) under that rule, and thereby provided God with the occasion to condemn sin and end its rule.[1] With the institution of another sphere, in which the Spirit influences behavior, it became possible for people to live righteously (8.4). The Temple cultus is, then, not a significant factor in this verse.

1 Corinthians 5.7

This verse is considered by most exegetes to be of a cultic nature.[2] Fitzer and Neuenzeit, however, have rejected this.[3] If Paul does have the cultus in mind here, he gives it little attention. The reference, if such it be, seems casual and uncharacteristic.[4] It has been suggested that the designation of Jesus as the Passover lamb was widespread in early Christianity,[5] a circumstance which might account for the terseness of 5.7b. But Friedrich points in denial to Jewish-Christian celebrations of Passover which failed to honor Jesus as the lamb, concentrating instead on eschatological expectation.[6]

The question of whether an actual celebration is at issue here has come in for dispute, as well. B. Lohse has argued that there was such a celebration.[7] He points out that what we know of the particular group that conducted it (called the

---

1 Althaus, *Römer* 76; Dodd, *Romans* 120; E. Gaugler, *Der Römerbrief* (SBG; 2 vols; Zürich: Zwingli Verlag, 1958) 1.263.

2 Conzelmann, *Outline* 70; N. Füglister, *Die Heilsbedeutung des Pascha* (StANT, 8; Munich: Kösel 1963) 19; A. Pluta, *Gottes Bundestreue* (SBS, 34; Stuttgart: Verlag Katholisches Bibelwerk, 1969) 74. On the Temple ritual, cf. Füglister, *Heilsbedeutung* 100-103.

3 Fitzer ('Der Ort' 172) believes that the Passover lamb cannot be understood as a propitiatory sacrifice, or even as a sacrifice at all, in the strict sense of the word. P. Neuenzeit, *Das Herrenmahl* (StANT, 1; Munich: Kösel, 1960) 166, maintains that 1 Cor. 5.7 cannot be used as evidence for a sacrificial interpretation of Jesus' death.

4 W. Bauer, *Das Johannesevangelium* (HNT, 6; 2nd edn; Tübingen: Mohr [Siebeck], 1925) 209; Bultmann, *Theology* 296; Friedrich, *Verkündigung* 47-49.

5 H. Conzelmann, *1 Corinthians: A Commentary on the First Epistle to the Corinthians* (trans. J.W. Leitch; bibliography and references by J.W. Dunkly; ed. G.W. MacRae; Philadelphia: Fortress, 1975) 99n49; J. Weiss, *Der erste Korintherbrief* (KEK, 5; 10th edn; Göttingen: Vandenhoeck & Ruprecht, 1925) 135.

6 Friedrich, *Verkündigung* 47-48.

7 B. Lohse, *Das Passafest det Quartadecimaner* (BFChTh 2nd series, 54; Gütersloh: Bertelsmann, 1953) 103-12; J. Jeremias, *The Eucharistic Words of Jesus* (trans. N. Perrin; New York: Scribner, 1966) 59-60, 122-25; E. Lohse, *Märtyrer* 142.

Quartadecimanians) goes back to Palestine.[1] 'However', he writes, 'we know nothing of another Christian Passover celebration at this time'. Therefore, the Passovers of the church at large and of the Quartadecimanians in particular are probably 'identical'. But this can hardly be regarded as conclusive, since the Quartadecimanian material is later and need not be connected with 1 Cor. 5.7b. Lohse also lists other, more specifically linguistic reasons for considering 5.7b a reference to an actual celebration. These are: (1) the Greek word for 'sacrificed' in 5.7b is a technical term for the slaughter of the Passover lamb; (2) the definite article before the Greek of 'our paschal lamb' shows that the designation of Jesus as the Passover lamb was presupposed as known; (3) the use of 'our' with 'paschal lamb' serves to distinguish the Christian Passover from the Jewish. But (1) technical terms can be used figuratively;[2] (2) that Jesus may have been known as the Passover lamb does not prove a real celebration—indeed, the definite article probably shows simply that the Passover lamb itself was a familiar item; (3) 'our' can indicate merely the close relation between Jesus and the believers.

Other exegetes have regarded an actual celebration as unlikely.[3] Weiss states that 'Let us, therefore, celebrate the festival' in 5.8 could indicate such a celebration, but since Paul's comments on leaven in 5.7a were figurative, this should probably be taken so, as well. Also if the celebration here were actual, then we would expect to find references to Passover when the Eucharist is mentioned; this is not, however, the case.[4] Finally, if there were a real celebration, the slaughter of Jesus the lamb would have to be thought of not as something past, but as contemporary. 'The passage would thus be speak-

---

1 B. Lohse, *Das Passafest* 74-76, 82-84.
2 Kuss, 'Die theologischen Grundgedanken', 1.296n78, denies that 1 Cor. 5.7 contains a technical term for the Passover lamb in the first place.
3 W. Bousset, 'Der erste Brief an die Korinther', *Die Schriften des Neuen Testaments* (ed. J. Weiss; 2nd edn; Göttingen: Vandenhoeck & Ruprecht, 1908) 91-92; H. Lietzmann, *An die Korinther I-II* (HNT, 9; ed. W.G. Kümmel; 4th edn; Tübingen: Mohr [Siebeck], 1949) 24.
4 Cf. J. Weiss, *Der erste Korintherbrief* (KEK, 5; 10th edn; Göttingen: Vandenhoeck & Ruprecht, 1925) 136, on the absence of a connection in Paul between the Passover and the Last Supper.

ing about a repetition of the slaughter, which is indeed unthinkable'.[1]

We can see, then, that 1 Cor. 5.7b offers only a brief allusion to the Temple cultus and is probably not a witness to any Christian adaptation of Hebrew cultic activitiy. When we look at the verse's context, we see further just how casual Paul's allusion to the Passover is. His topic in 1 Cor. 5 is immorality in the community. In verses 5-6, he compares the community to dough, and immorality to leaven. Verse 7a contains Paul's characteristic juxtaposition of the imperative ('cleanse out') and the indicative 'you really are').[2] This juxtaposition occurs at a number of crucial points in Paul. Rudolf Bultmann has identified it as relying on the conceptuality of aeons or cosmic dominions. The indicative, he says, refers to those who have been released from the power of sin.[3] This release is not open ended, but imposes an obligation to live in obedience to the new lord, Christ (hence the imperative). As Bultmann says, '... the life conferred by baptism must prove itself in the present by its freedom from the power of sin ...'[4] When Paul tells the Corinthians that they are unleavened, he means that they are no longer under the power of sin, and when he admonishes them to clean out the old leaven, he asks them to behave in a manner appropriate to their new lord. The mention of Christ's sacrifice as the paschal lamb, coming directly after the indicative, is simply a way of referring to the founding event on which that indicative is based, while at the same time maintaining the figure of speech begun in v. 6. Under consideration here are not the expiatory, sacrificial implications of Christ's death,[5] but the latter as the turning-point of the aeons.[6]

That Paul is thinking in terms of aeons/cosmic dominions/ spheres of existence is shown by the succeeding verses. There he sets Christians over against the 'world' (*kosmos*). Those in

---

1 Weiss, *Korintherbrief* 136.
2 Cf. R. Bultmann, 'The Problem of Ethics in the Writings of Paul', *The Old and New Man* (Richmond, Va.: John Knox, 1967) 7-32.
3 Bultmann, *Theology* 330-33.
4 Bultmann, *Theology* 333.
5 Fitzer, 'Der Ort' 172.
6 Beker, *Paul the Apostle* 191.

the 'world' he calls 'outsiders', suggesting that they and Christians live in different dominions or spheres of existence. Then, in 6.2, Paul refers to the fate of these two spheres. At the end, Christians 'will judge the world'. The thinking here is essentially apocalyptic, not sacrificial and cultic.

1 Corinthians 10.14-22

This passage, thought to have been influenced by tradition,[1] refers to Hebrew (10.18) and Hellenistic (10.19-21) cultic practices.[2]

Some, however, have suggested the Hebrew practices at issue here represent not the Temple cultus but rather the sacrifice before the golden calf.[3] That Paul refers to idolatry in 10.19, and that he has just used the golden calf as an example of such behaviour (10.7-8) are facts which at least open the possibility.

But even if Paul does have the Temple cultus in mind at 10.18, he seems uninterested in playing its particulars off against Jesus' death. As just noted, he compares the Eucharist to *both* Hebrew and Hellenistic liturgies in order to warn against idolatry.[4] The point of comparison is that participation in Temple cultus, Hellenistic ceremonies, and the Eucharist binds one to the lord of those rites. Hebrews who eat the sacrifices become 'partners' in the altar dedicated to God. Christians who partake of the 'table of demons' would provoke Christ to a jealous reaction against such misplaced loyalty. As for the Eucharist itself, Paul's language makes it clear that his concern is with a lord–subject relationship established by each of the types of ritual he mentions. The cup is a 'participation' (*koinonia*) in Christ's blood, and the bread is a 'participation'

---

1 E. Käsemann, 'The Pauline Doctrine of the Lord's Supper', *Essays on New Testament Themes* (SBT, 41; trans. W.J. Montague; Naperville, Ill.: Allenson 1964) 109-10; C. Wolff, *Der erste Brief des Paulus an die Korinther* (ThHK, 7; part 2; Berlin: Evangelische Verlagsanstalt, 1982) 50-52.

2 Cf. H.-J. Klauck, *1 Korintherbrief* (NEcB, 7; Würzburg: Echter Verlag, 1984) 258-72.

3 Cf. G. Bornkamm, 'Lord's Supper and Church in Paul', *Early Christian Experience* (New York: Harper, 1969) 159n60.

4 For a critique of the downplaying of these comparisons, cf. S. Aalen, 'Das Abendmahl als Opfermahl im Neuen Testament', *NovT* 6 (1963) 128-30.

(*koinonia*) in his body.[1] (There has been some debate among German exegetes on whether *Teilhabe* [participation] or *Gemeinschaft* [community] is indicated here,[2] but a linkage in some sort of lord–subject relationship is meant in any case.)

It has been pointed out that Paul speaks here of participation in the sacrifice as well as in subjection to a supernatural lord.[3] So much is evident, but that does not obviate the fact that being bound to a supernatural lord is Paul's predominant consideration. Participation in that lord's sacrifice leads to this binding: '... the eating of the bread and the drinking from the cup, performed communally, convey personal partnership with the crucified and risen Christ through participation in his body and blood ...'[4] The reason Paul must warn against involvement in pagan sacrifices is beacuse they lead to partnership with demons.[5] While Hebrew sacrifices are not, of course, demonic, the same point about binding holds true: those who perform and partake of them become bound to the god of that altar.[6]

It can thus be said that Paul's interest in all the cultic practices he mentions centers around the issues of lordship and the consequent unity of the lord's subjects. Indeed, if 1 Cor. 10.14-22 is concerned with 'cultic' matters, it is so only to the extent that these matters apply alike to the Christian Eucharist, Hebrew rites, and pagan feasts. That is, Paul does not address himself here to the peculiar fashion in which *koinonia* is created between believers and Christ by the Eucharist. What he does address is the lordship established and the unity created by any such ritual, be it Christian, Jewish, or pagan. At no

1 The great majority of exegetes agree that Paul has reversed the traditional order of bread-cup so as to talk about the bread in 1 Cor. 10.17. Cf. e.g. Bornkamm, 'Lord's Supper' 143; Käsemann, 'Pauline Doctrine' 110.

2 Conzelmann, *Corinthians* 171, labels this choice a false alternative. Cf. also Klauck, *Korintherbrief* 73.

3 Aalen, 'Abendmahl' 129-30.

4 Klauck, *Korinther* 73. Cf. also W.F. Orr and J.A. Walther, *1 Corinthians* (AB 32; Garden City, New York: Doubleday, 1976) 251-52.

5 Cf. P. Bachmann, *Der erste Brief des Paulus an die Korinther* (4th edn; Leipzig: Deichert, 1936) 339; H.-J. Klauck, *Herrenmahl und hellenistischer Kult* (Neutestamentliche Abhandlungen, new series 15; Münster: Aschendorff, 1982) 284.

6 On 'altar' as a pious circumlocution for 'God', cf. e.g. H. Gressmann, ῾Η κοινωνία τῶν δαιμονίων', *ZNW* 20 (1921) 224.

point in this passage does he indicate that Christian *koinonia* is different from that of Jews or pagans.[1] He does deny that idols are anything, but in verses 20-21 he implies that pagans are partners with demons just as Christians are partners with Christ. Paul's lack of interest here in the specifics of cultic activity lets him feel free to change the traditional formula in verse 16. It is not ritual correctness he is after at this point, but the emphasis on unity which his change achieves.[2] If Christians are genuinely to have Christ as their lord, they must be united with their fellow believers and with Christ himself.

We find, then, that as with the other passages we have examined, the Temple cultus seems not to play a formative role in the development of Paul's soteriology here. If Paul is referring to the cultus at all, it is only as one more example in his argument agains idolatry, and it does not constitute a significant influence.

1 Corinthians 11.14-26

This passage is marked as received material by Paul himself. The only qestion is the method of the reception: tradition,[3] revelation,[4] or some combination thereof.[5] The consensus of exegetes regards the first as most likely.

Those who point to a sacrificial type in the Old Testament for this passage generally choose either the Passover[6] or the

---

1   Alfred F. Loisy, *The Birth of the Christian Religion* (trans. L.P. Jacks; New Hyde Park, New York: University Books, 1962) 247.

2   Cf. E. Schweizer, *The Lord's Supper according to the New Testament* (trans. J.M. Davis; Philadelphia: Fortress, 1967) 36. Schweizer notes there that 'for Paul this body [in vv. 16-17] is significant only as the sphere of the sovereignty of the Lord and the realm of his blessings'.

3   E.-B. Allo, *Première Épître aux Corinthiens* (2nd edn; Paris: Librairie Lecoffre, 1956) 277; R. Pesch, *Das Abendmahl und Jesu Todverständnis* (QD, 80; Freiburg, Basel, and Vienna: Herder, 1978) 54-57, 66-69; E. Schürmann, *Der Einsetzungsbericht* (NA, 20; Münster: Aschendorff, 1955) 7-14.

4   H. Lietzmann, *Mass and Lord's Supper* (trans. D.H.G. Reeve; Leiden: Brill, 1979) 208, 208n1.

5   O. Cullmann, ' "KYRIOS" as Designation for the Oral Tradition concerning Jesus', *SJT* 3 (1950) 189; A.J.B. Higgins, *The Lord's Supper in the New Testament* (SBT, 6; London: SCM, 1956) 28.

6   M. Barth, *Das Abendmahl* (ThS, 18; Zürich: Zollikon, 1945) 13-15; R.H. Kennet, *The Last Supper* (Cambridge: Heffer, 1921) 38.

rites described in Ex. 24.5-6.[1] The first of these is improbable because, as Bornkamm says, 'the accounts of the institution [of the Last Supper] themselves contain hardly any relation to the Passover at all'.[2] Regarding the second, it is to be said that, whatever the concern of the traditional kernel, Paul seems much more interested in covenant than in a sacrifice which established it.[3] He fails to develop or even specifically refer to any aspect of sacrifice.[4] His real point here is the unity of the congregation under Jesus' lordship.[5] Conzelmann writes: 'It is a case of the upbuilding or destroying of the community as such ...'[6] The problem Paul is dealing with is that there are 'divisions' when the Corinthians gather (11.18). This fact makes it impossible for the Lord's supper genuinely to be celebrated (11.20). Such celebration is possible only if the body is discerned (11.29), that is, only if it be understood that the sacrament signifies the lord who has died for the community[7] and welded it into a unit. That this death has in fact brought the believers into a realm which Christ rules as lord is shown by 11.30. To partake of the Lord's Supper improperly is to risk illness or even death at the ruler's hands. Referring back to the previous chapter in 1 Corinthians, Käsemann makes this point clearly: 'Wherever we do not truly partake of him and allow ourselves to be incorporated into his kingdom, according to 10.22 we are provoking the *Kyrios* to display his power of

1　Conzelmann, *Corinthians* 199; Lietzmann, *Korinther* 57.

2　Bornkamm, 'Lord's Supper' 132. Jeremias has been the foremost champion of the link between the Lord's Supper and Passover. For a detailed refutation of his argument, cf. R.D. Richardson, 'A Further Inquiry into Eucharistic Origins with Special Reference to New Testament Problems', in Lietzmann, *Mass* 625-40.

3　Davies, *Paul and Rabbinic Judaism* 253; cf. also J. Behm's insistence that the Eucharist in Paul is not a sacrificial meal ('θύω', *TDNT* 3 [1965] 184).

4　Cf. J. Betz's demonstration that the linkage of 'body' (*soma*) and 'blood' (*haima*) is not used by the Septuagint in sacrificial contexts, *Die Realpräsenz des Leibes und Blutes Jesu im Abendmahl nach dem Neuen Testament*, vol. 2, part 1 of *Die Eucharistie in der Zeit der Griechischen Väter* (Freiburg, Basel, and Vienna: Herder, 1961) 21n80. Cf. also Neuenzeit, *Das Herrenmahl* 165.

5　S. Scott Bartchy, 'Table Fellowship with Jesus and the "Lord's Meal" at Corinth', *Increase in Learning: Essays in Honor of James G. Van Buren* (eds. R.O. Owens, Jr. and B.E. Hamm; Manhatten, Kansas: Manhatten Christian College, 1979) 47; Bornkamm, 'Lord's Supper' 139.

6　Conzelmann, *Corinthians* 193.

7　Barrett, *Romans* 274-75, considers the various alternatives and concludes that the body in question is indeed that of Christ. Cf. also F.F. Bruce, *1 and 2 Corinthians* (London: Marshall, Morgan & Scott, 1971) 115.

judgment and death and to meet us as the one stronger than we. It is of just this encounter that, according to v. 30, the frightened Corinthians are witnesses'.[1]

Once more we have found that the Temple cultus plays only a minor role in Paul's soteriology, and that his thought really centers around the church as an entity united under Christ's lordship by his death.

Conclusion

This chapter has shown that the Temple cultus does not possess an important function in Pauline soteriology. Time after time, allusions to the Temple cultus have been seen to reside in passages whose substantive concerns are the old aeon of Sin, the new aeon of Christ's lordship, and Jesus' death as the turning point between them. Paul was, of course, familiar with the Temple cultus and referred to it a number of times. But his understanding of Jesus' saving death depends much less on sacrifice or cultus than on aeons or spheres of existence.

1 Käsemann, 'Pauline Doctrine' 125.

Chapter 2

PAUL'S DOCTRINE OF SALVATION
AND THE SUFFERING SERVANT (ISAIAH 52–53)

Introduction

Along with the Temple cultus (covered in Chapter 1), the Suffering Servant of Isaiah 52–53 has received considerable attention as a possible influence on Paul's understanding of Jesus' saving death. This chapter will determine the likelihood of such influence. As in Chapter 1, the procedure will be to treat each relevant passage in turn.

Romans 3.25

There is little comment on links between this verse and Isaiah. However, Jeremias asserts that the reference to God's 'passing over' (*paresis*) of sins echoes Isa. 53.4, 5, and 12.[1] This is curious, since the phrase in Rom. 3.25 does not express vicarious benefit, as do the Isaianic verses. Jeremias fails to address this disparity in meaning. Nor does he give any reason why the reference to a 'passing over' of sins should be attached to the Servant.

Cranfield states that the possible influence of Isa. 53.10 on Paul's view of Christ as *hilasterion* 'deserves to be seriously considered', but then fails to consider it at all.[2] Since the Septuagint version of Isa. 53.10 does not contain the word *hilasterion*, it is difficult to see a connection between that verse and Rom. 3.25.[3]

1 J. Jeremias, 'παῖς θεοῦ' *TDNT* 5 (1967) 710, 710nn434-35.
2 Cranfield, *Romans* 1.218.
3 Cf. Käsemann, *Romans* 97; U. Schnelle, *Gerechtigkeit und Christusgegenwart* (Göttingen: Vandenhoeck & Ruprecht, 1973) 200n322.

Romans 4.25a

Rom. 4.25 is judged to be traditional by most exegetes.[1] Reasons include: (1) the introductory 'who', (2) the parallelism; (3) the passive form of the verbs (often found in traditional material); (4) the occurrence, uncommon for Paul, of the Greek word translated here as 'justification', (5) the plural of the Greek word translated as 'trespasses' (again, uncommon for Paul); (6) the un-Pauline connection of Christ's resurrection with our justification.[2]

Discussion regarding a link between Rom. 4.25a and the Servant generally centers around the similarity of the former to the end of Isa. 53.12.[3] When a type of text is mentioned at all, it is usually the Septuagint, for the end of Isa. 53.12 in that version runs as follows: 'he was given up (*paradidomi*) for their sins (*hamartia*)'. This is similar to Rom. 4.25a, which reads: 'who was put to death (*paradidomi*) for our trespasses (*paraptoma*)'. One is still left, however, with the difficulty that Rom. 4.25a uses 'trespasses' instead of 'sins'.[4] Thus, Schnelle and Strecker deny that a connection can be established on the basis of so little common language,[5] and Cranfield makes clear just how frequent *paradidomi* is in the New Testament.[6]

---

1 The following, among many, assert that Rom. 4.25 is traditional: Bultmann, *Theology* 46-47, 82; Conzelmann, *Outline* 70; E. Fascher, *Jesaja 53 in christlicher und jüdischer Sicht* (AVTRW 4; Berlin: Evangelische Verlagsanstalt, n.d.) 11n6.

2 See the similar collections of these reasons in W. Popkes, *Christus Traditus* (AThANT, 49; Zürich & Stuttgart: Zwingli, 1967) 194-95; Schlier, *Römerbrief* 136.

3 Cf. e.g. G. Delling, 'The Significance of the Resurrection of Jesus for Faith in Jesus Christ', *The Significance of the Message of the Resurrection for Faith in Jesus Christ* (SBT, 8; second series; trans D.M. Barton and R.A. Wilson; ed. C.F.D. Moule; Naperville, Ill.; Alec R. Allenson, 1968) 79; K.H. Schelkle, *Die Passion Jesu in der Verkündigung des Neuen Testaments* (Heidelberg: Kerle, 1949) 71, 95, 193.

4 S. Lyonnet, 'Péché', *Dictionnaire de la bible. Supplément* (eds. L. Pirot, et al.; Paris: Letouzey & Ané, 1966) 495, proposes that Paul has changed *hamartia* to *paraptoma*. But this is difficult to understand in light of Paul's willingness to use *hamartia* in a traditional phrase at 1 Cor. 15.3; cf. H. Patsch, 'Zum alttestamentlichen Hintergrund von Römer 4.25 und I. Petrus 2.24', *ZNW* 60 (1969) 276.

5 G. Strecker, 'Befreiung und Rechtfertigung. Zur Stellung der Rechtfertigungslehre in der Theologie des Paulus', *Rechtfertigung* (eds. J. Friedrich, W. Pöhlmann, and P. Stuhlmacher; Tübingen: Mohr [Siebeck]; Göttingen: Vandenhoeck & Ruprecht, 1976) 503n86.

6 Cranfield, *Romans* 1.251. See also p. 43n1 and p. 44n6 below.

Jeremias,[1] Klappert,[2] and Perrin[3] have traced Rom. 4.25a to
the Targum, or Aramaic translation, of Isa. 53.6. But Patsch[4]
has pointed out that, in view of the meaning of Isa. 53.5
Targum (which concerns the Temple), this is improbable.
Patsch himself has gone on to suggest that Isa. 53.12b Septuagint and Rom. 4.25a are 'independent translations of a non-
Masoretic text' represented by 1QIsa a-b 53.12, from the Dead
Sea Scrolls.[5] But this still leaves difficulties over the Hebrew
verb being translated by *paradidomi*.[6]

In sum, it can be said that Isa. 53.12 LXX provides the closest
link with Rom. 4.25a. Both contain the verb *paradidomi* and
associate the event it signifies with some wrongdoing by persons other than the victim. This provides enough evidence to
say that there may well be an allusion to Isaiah 53 here.
Nevertheless, it is unlikely that Rom. 4.25a represents anything approaching a full-blown or elaborate 'Servant theology'
(in German, *Gottesknechttheologie*). There was little or no
reflection on the Servant as a salvific figure in Judaism at this
time.[7] This fact indicates that more clarity would have been
necessary here for anyone to get the point.

One could object to this conclusion on the ground that Paul
is, in a sense, 'showing off' his knowledge of the Old Testament
text and his facility in adapting it to Christ. But the lack of
Jewish, soteriological reflection on the Servant would still
leave one with the question: showing off to whom? Is it plausi-
ble that, unlike contemporary Judaism, the early church *did*
engage in widespread reflection on the Servant as a salvific

---

1 J. Jeremias, 'Artikelloses Χριστός. Zur Ursprache von 1 Cor 15.3b-5', *ZNW* 57
   (1966) 211-215; *idem*, *TDNT* 5.706n397.
2 B. Klappert, 'Zur Frage des semitischen oder griechischen Urtextes von 1 Kor.
   XV.3-5' *NTS* 13 (1966-67) 168-73.
3 N. Perrin, 'The Use of (παρα)διδόναι in Connection with the Passion of Jesus in
   the New Testament', *Der Ruf Jesu und die Antwort der Gemeinde* (ed. E. Lohse
   with C. Burchard & B. Schaller; Göttingen: Vandenhoeck & Ruprecht, 1970) 211.
4 Patsch, 'Zum alttestamentlichen Hintergrund' 275-76.
5 Patsch, 'Zum alttestamentlichen Hintergrund' 277-78.
6 Cf. Schnelle, *Gerechtigkeit* 202n354.
7 J.M. van Cangh, '"Mort pour nos péchés selon les Écritures" (1 Co 15.3b) Une
   référence à Isaie 53?' *Revue Théologique du Louvain* 1/2 (1970) 198; M.D. Hooker,
   Jesus and the Servant (London: SPCK, 1959) 53-61; S.H.T. Page, 'The Suffering
   Servant between the Testaments', *NTS* 31 (1985) 481-84, 486-88; S.K. Williams,
   Jesus' Death 111-20.

figure? If so, this could account for why the Servant did not
have to be explicitly mentioned at Rom. 4.25a: the comparison
between him and Christ was so familiar as to render such
explicitness unnecessary.[1] But without any preparation in
terms of Jewish tradition, the church would have had to be
remarkably creative in order to arrive at this interpretation so
quickly and so extensively. Hengel argues that divine
intervention did in fact render this possible.[2] Considered historically, however, the evidence will not support such a
conclusion.

On the question of whether any 'servant theology' has been
utilized by Paul we can feel more secure, for the answer is no.
Five reasons can be offered as to why this is the case: (1) it is
strange that Paul, just after discussing an Old Testament
figure like Abraham (4.1-23), and shortly before discussing
another one like Adam (5.12-19), finds himself unable to refer
more clealy to the Servant; (2) 5.3-5 constitutes an exhortation
to endure suffering, a subject to which the example of the
Servant might fruitfully have been applied, if it were actually
in Paul's mind; (3) in the next verse (5.1), Paul says that now
'we have peace with God'; this adumbrates the language of
reconciliation between enemies in 5.9-10 (see above, pp. 27-
28), and stands within Paul's aeon theology rather than in a
'servant theology'; (4) similarly, the statement in 5.2 that,
through Christ, 'we have obtained access to this grace in
which we stand' suggests a transferral from standing in one
realm or aeon to standing in another; (5) when Paul comes
again to discuss Jesus' death in connection with 'trespasses'
(5.15-20), he does so not in terms of the Servant, but of the
aeons which Adam and Christ represent.

All these reasons lend credence to the proposition that 4.25a,
if it is an allusion to Isaiah 53, remains isolated in its context[3]
and does not contribute to any larger pattern.[4] A 'servant
theology' is not in evidence here.

---

1 Hengel, *The Atonement* 60.
2 Hengel, *The Atonement* 60.
3 Schnelle, *Gerchtigkeit* 72.
4 Käsemann, *Romans* 128; cf. D. Juel, 'The Image of the Servant-Christ in the New
   Testament', *SWJT* 21 (1979) 15, 17-18.

Romans 8.32a

Rom. 8.32a, sometimes considered traditional,[1] is said to reflect Isa. 53.6 LXX or 53.12 LXX because it contains the phrase 'gave him up for us all'.[2] Schweizer, however, is unconvinced, maintaining that the Greek verb translated as 'gave up' is very common and need not be tied specifically to Isaiah 53.[3] Most commentators simply ignore the suggestion.[4]

Although Rom. 8.32a does resemble Isa. 53.6 LXX, there are considerable differences, as well. The latter contains the same Greek verb translated in Rom. 8.32a as 'gave up', but instead of 'for us all' we find 'for our sins'. As for Isa. 53.12 LXX, it reads 'he was given up because of their sins', and in the Greek has no language identical to Rom. 8.32a. Any connection between Rom. 8.32a and Isaiah must rest on a single word in Isa. 53.6 LXX and on the general idea of someone being given up for others. This means that, as with the other passages we have examined, any link must remain implicit rather than explicit. Hence, it is doubtful that a 'servant theology' is at issue here, since the same lack of soteriological reflection on the Servant noted above[5] would seem to have dictated more explicitness.

As for the use Paul makes of any echo of Isaiah in Rom. 8.32a, the context shows that there is none. Rom. 8.32a stands in a section which is strongly influenced by apocalypticism. (This in itself does not preclude use of the Servant, since the latter could appear as part of an apocalypticized format. It will be seen, however that Paul does not in fact incorporate the Servant as a component of his apocalyptic theology.) At Rom. 8.18, Paul says he considers 'the sufferings of this present time' insignificant in comparison 'with the glory that is to be

---

1 R. Deichgräber, *Gotteshymnus und Christushymnus in der frühen Christenheit* (SUNT, 5; Göttingen: Vandenhoeck & Ruprecht 1967) 112; H. Paulsen, *Überlieferung und Auslegung in Römer* 8 (WMANT, 43; Neukirchen-Vluyn: Neukirchener Verlag, 1974) 161.

2 Cranfield, *Romans* 1.436 (Isa. 53.12); Jeremias, *TDNT* 5.710 (Isa. 53.6).

3 E. Schweizer, *Lordship and Discipleship* (SBT, 28; Naperville, Ill.; Alec R. Allenson, 1960) 50n2. Cf. p. 40n6 above and p. 44n6 below.

4 E.g. M.-L. Gubler, *Die frühesten Deutungen des Todes Jesu* (OBO, 15; Schweiz: Freiburg; Göttingen: Vandenhoeck & Ruprecht, 1977) 212-14; W. Kramer, *Christ, Lord, Son of God* (SBT, 50; Naperville, Ill.: Alec R. Allenson, 1966) section 26a.

5 See above, p. 41n7.

revealed to us'.[1] In encouraging his readers to await confidently this coming glory, Paul assures them that their victory is as good as won. Rom. 8.32 is part of this assurance. A few verses later (Rom. 8.35), Paul refers to the eschatological trials[2] which, however, cannot separate believers from Christ. Then, in verse 38, there appear the 'angels', 'principalities', 'things present', 'things to come', and 'powers' so characteristic of apocalypticism.[3] As Käsemann points out, only apocalypticism describes reality in this way.[4]

1 Corinthians 11.23

It is sometimes held that the Greek verb translated as 'betrayed' reflects Isaiah 53.[5] Others deny this.[6] Most commentators ignore the matter.[7]

All that can be said for sure, it seems, is that once more Paul takes no notice of whatever catchword connection there may be here. As seen in Chapter 1, Paul's concern here is for the unity of the church under Christ's lordship, an issue more akin to the aeon categories observed so often above than to a 'servant theology'.

1 Corinthians 15.3

1 Cor. 15.3, which Paul cites as traditional,[8] is widely believed to be a reference to Isaiah 52–53 since, as E. Lohse says, 'at no other place in the Old Testament is the representative power

---

1 For the apocalyptic tone of this verse and of the section it introduces, see Michel, *Römer* 264-66; Wilckens, *Römer* 2.151.

2 Käsemann, *Romans* 249-50; Schlier, *Römerbrief* 279.

3 Käsemann, *Romans* 250-52; Michel, *Römer* 285; von der Osten-Sacken, *Römer* 848nn1-2.

4 Käsemann, *Romans* 251.

5 Conzelmann, *Corinthians* 197n44.

6 Davies, *Paul and Palestinian Judaism* 250. Cf. also J. Behm, 'διαθήκη', *TDNT* 2 (1964) 133; Popkes, *Christus Traditus* 209; Schweizer, *Lordship* 50n2.

7 Barrett, *Corinthians* 266; Klauck, *Korintherbrief* 82.

8 On the pre-Pauline character of 1 Cor. 15.3-5, see A. Seeberg, *Der Katechismus der Urchristenheit* (Leipzig: A. Deichert, 1903) 45-58, who provided the first thorough examination of these verses as a fixed, pre-Pauline tradition. Cf. also, *inter alia*, J. Murphy-O'Connor, 'Tradition and Redaction in 1 Cor. 15.3-7', *CBQ* 43 (1981) 582-84 and the literature cited there.

of suffering and death spoken of so abundantly'.[1] Yet this consensus has not gone unquestioned. Some insist that the evidence is too slight for the issue to be decided.[2] Others maintain that 'in accordance with the scriptures' simply means the Hebrew Bible as a whole.[3] Finally, it can be asked how this terse phrase can mean Isa. 52–53 when nowhere in postexilic Judaism can be found an explicit soteriological reference to those chapters.[4]

All of these challenges have merit. Even the most fervent advocates of the distinct positions which have been taken must admit that the evidence is, indeed, insufficient for certainty to be arrived at. Likewise, it must be acknowledged that the Greek does indeed mean 'according to the writings' or 'according to the scriptures', without singling out a specific passage. Such specificity can only be implicit. But how could an author at the dawn of Christianity assume readers would catch an implicit reference to Isaiah 53 in such a formula? As for Paul, how could he assume such a reference would be comprehended by his congregation at Corinth when he rarely, if ever, uses it elsewhere?

Another problem in connecting 1 Cor. 15.3 and Isaiah 53 concerns the attempt to establish original wording. Did the latter accord with the Isaiah 53 of the Masoretic text, the Septuagint, or the Targums? Jeremias wrote in the third edition of *Die Abendmahlsworte Jesu* that 'with certainty' ('mit Sicherheit') the kerygmatic core of 1 Cor. 15.3ff. came from the earliest, Aramaic speaking community.[5] Conzelmann then argued that the formula is actually closer to the Septua-

---

1 E. Lohse, *Märtyrer* 114. Cf. C. Bussmann, 'Christus starb für unsere Sünden', *Biblische Randbemerkungen* (eds. H. Merklein and J. Lange, 2nd edn; Würzburg: Echter Verlag, 1974) 343; J. Kloppenborg, 'An Analysis of the Pre-Pauline Formula 1 Cor. 15.3b-5 in Light of Some Recent Literature', *CBQ* 40 (1978) 364; K. Lehmann, *Auferweckt am dritten Tag nach der Schrift* (QD, 38; Freiburg, Basel and Vienna: Herder, 1968) 79, 248.

2 E.g. K Wengst, *Christologische Formeln und Lieder des Urchristentums* (Gütersloh: Mohn, 1972) 95, 100.

3 J. Kremer, *Das älteste Zeugnis von Auferstehung Christi*, (SB 17; Stuttgart: Katholisches Bibelwerk, 1967) 35, 36n24; G. Schrenk, 'γραφή', *TDNT* 1 (1964) 752.

4 See above, n16.

5 J. Jeremias, *The Eucharistic Words of Jesus* (trans N. Perrin; New York: Scribner, 1966) 103; *Die Abendmahlsworte Jesu* (3rd edn; Göttingen: Vandenhoeck & Ruprecht, 1960) 97.

gint.[1] Subsequently, in the fourth edition of *Die Abendmahls-worte Jesu*, Jeremias claimed only that the passage 'probably' ('wahrscheinlich') goes back to the oldest, Aramaic speaking community.[2] He also states in this edition that 'according to the scriptures' is an 'Hellenistic-Jewish-Christian addition'.[3] The debate has continued,[4] but Wengst's conclusion seems correct: 'Considerations which are won from the linguistic structure of the formula neither can make the adoption of an original, Semitic text sufficiently probable, nor are capable of excluding such an adoption with certainty'.[5]

In sum,[6] we can say only that 1 Cor. 15.3 may contain faint or implicit echoes of Isaiah 53. Because the formula is not more specific, because there was no tradition of such references to Isaiah 53, and because the formula does not match any known precursor text, it is impossible to say more.

When the context of 1 Cor. 15.3 is considered, even this possible significance of Servant soteriology begins to fade, and once again aeon categories come to the fore. H. Boers has stated that 1 Cor. 15 'is the locus classicus in the writings of Paul in which we have ... an "unveiling" as an interpretive proclamation of the concluding events of this eon ...'[7] Paul's purpose in this chapter is to affirm the truth of the resurrection of the dead (v. 12). If there is no such resurrection, then Christ has not been raised (v. 13). And if Christ has not been raised, then no one has been saved (v. 17). In v. 17, Paul uses the plural 'in your sins' rather than a singular reference

---

1 H. Conzelmann, 'On the Analysis of the Confessional Formula in 1 Corinthians 15.3-5', *Int* 20 (1966) 15-25.

2 J. Jeremias, *Die Abendmahlsworte Jesu* (4th edn; Göttingen: Vandenhoeck & Ruprecht, 1967) 97.

3 Jeremias, *Abendmahlsworte*, 4th edn 98.

4 See the literature cited by Friedrich, *Verkündigung* 22-23n47 and S.K. Williams, *Jesus' Death* 220n49.

5 Wengst, *Christologische Formeln* 98. In fairness, it should be noted that Jeremias traces 1 Cor. 15.3ff. back to the earliest stratum of the church not so much because of linguistic considerations as because of Paul's claim that his kerygma and the apostles' are the same, *Eucharistic Words* 103.

6 Because it is a problem involving the history of the verse and our concern here is with Paul himself, we will not be considering the question of the possible, original independence of 'for our sins' and 'in accordance with the scriptures'. For debate on the issue see *inter alia* F. Hahn, *The Titles of Jesus in Christology* (LL; New York and Cleveland: World Publishing Co., 1969) 177-79.

7 H.W. Boers, 'Apocalyptic Eschatology in 1 Corinthians 15', *Int* 21 (1967) 52.

to sin as a power. Presumably he is here hearkening back to 1 Cor. 15.3.[1] However, the issue of spheres of power arises in verses 18 and 19, where Paul's characteristic 'in Christ' appears. Moreover, in vv. 21-22, there appears the Adam-Christ typology which is spelled out at Romans 5.[2] Death came into the world through the first man, and those who are 'in Adam' are subject to it.[3] But those 'in Christ' will become alive. Death is clearly conceived as a power in v. 26, where it is called 'the last enemy to be destroyed',[4] reference having just been made to 'rule', 'authority' and 'power' in v. 24.[5]

1 Corinthians 15 contains hints of a 'servant theology' overshadowed by the concept of aeons or spheres of power. Whatever allusion to Isaiah 53 may be contained in 1 Cor. 15.3 is not developed. The Suffering Servant is not a real concern for Paul at this point.

Galatians 1.4a

This passage, which is considered traditional,[6] is traced to Isaiah 53 because it contains the phrase 'who gave himself for our sins'. The Isaianic verses at issue are 53.5 LXX,[7] 53.5 MT,[8] 53.5 Tg,[9] 53.6 LXX,[10] 53.10 MT,[11] 53.12LXX,[12] and 53.12 Tg.[13] However, none of these various candidates provides a complete linguistic correspondence with Gal. 1.4 and, as Betz

---

1 Conzelmann, *Corinthians* 266, C. Wolff, *Der erste Brief des Paulus an die Korinther* (ThHK, 7; part 2; Berlin: Evangelische Verlagsanstalt, 1982) 174.

2 Conzelmann, *Corinthians* 269n52.

3 Conzelmann, *Corinthians* 268–69.

4 Brandenburger, *Adam und Christus* 71.

5 Cf. von der Osten-Sacken, *Römer* 8 480-81.

6 B.H. Brinsmead, *Galatians—Dialogical Response to Opponents* (SBLDS, 65; Chico, CA: Scholars Press, 1982) 59; F. Mussner, *Der Galaterbrief* (HThK, 9; Freiburg, Basel & Vienna: Herder, 1974) 50.

7 K. Romaniuk, 'L'Origine des Formules Pauliniennes "Le Christ s'est livré pour nous", "Le Christ nous a aimés et s'est livré pour nous"' *NovT* 5 (1962) 58.

8 Romaniuk, 'L'Origine' 58.

9 Romaniuk, 'L'Origine' 58.

10 H. Schlier, *Der Brief an die Galater* (KEK 7; 14th edn; Göttingen: Vandenhoeck & Ruprecht, 1971) 32.

11 Jeremias, *TDNT* 5.710.

12 F.F. Bruce, *The Epistle to the Galatians* (NIGTC; Grand Rapids: Eerdmans, 1982) 75.

13 Jeremias, *TDNT* 5.710.

points out, Isaiah 53 offers no parallel to the motif of self-sacrifice.[1]

More importantly, in Gal. 1.4b Paul makes explicit use of aeon categories to interpret Jesus' saving death. By this death, Jesus delivered us 'from the present evil aeon'. Despite attempts to allegorize[2] or downplay[3] their role, there can be little doubt that Paul is explicating the significance of the death by means of apocalyptically conceived aeons.[4]

Galatians 2.20b

There is some speculation that v. 20 is traditional.[5] The phrase 'who ... gave himself for me' has provoked comparisons with Isa. 53.6 LXX,[6] 53.10 MT,[7] 53.12 MT,[8] and 53.12 Tg.[9] These linguistic echoes are slight at best, a fact which accounts for their being ignored by most commentators.[10]

That such neglect is justified is suggested by the context. There is no indication of a 'servant theology'. Instead, the mystery religions[11] and baptism[12] are the two backgrounds against which v. 20 (along with the closely connected v. 19) is most commonly seen. Mystery religions will be dealt with in Chapter 4. As for baptism, Betz points out that at the only place in Galatians where Paul mentions baptism (3.27), he does not speak of Jesus' death. Conversely, he can speak of dying with

---

1 H.D. Betz, *Galatians: A Commentary on Paul's Letter to the Churches in Galatia* (Hermeneia; Philadelphia: Fortress, 1979) 42n55.

2 C.B. Cousar, *Galatians* (Atlanta: John Knox, 1982) 17-18.

3 D. Guthrie, *Galatians* (The Century Bible; new series; London: Nelson, 1969) 60; Schlier, *Galater* 33-34.

4 A. Oepke, *Der Brief des Paulus an die Galater* (ThHK, 9; ed. J. Rohde; Berlin: Evangelische Verlagsanstalt, 1973) 45-46. Paul has, of course, modified his received apocalyptic notions to the extent of regarding the evil aeon's power as already fractured. Cf. H. Sasse, 'αἰών', *TDNT* 1 (1963) 207.

5 Kramer, *Christ*, section 26b; Mussner, *Galaterbrief* 183.

6 Bruce, *Galatians* 146; Hahn, *Titles* 61.

7 Jeremias, *TDNT* 5.170; Romaniuk, 'L'Origine' 57.

8 Bruce, *Galatians* 146.

9 Jeremias, *TDNT* 5.710.

10 K. Kertelge, *'Rechtfertigung' bei Paulus* (NA new series 3; Münster: Aschendorff, 1967) 239-42; Schlier, *Galater* 101-103.

11 Cf. Betz, *Galatians* 124n93; Oepke, *Galater* 95n252.

12 E.g. H.-W. Beyer and P. Althaus, *Der Brief an die Galater* (NTD, 8; 10th edn; Göttingen: Vandenhoeck & Ruprecht, 1965) 21.

Christ (5.24; 6.24), while making no reference to baptism. These considerations, together with the fact that Romans 6 is the only passage where Paul interprets baptism as death/ resurrection with Christ, cause Betz to conclude that such an interpretation must be secondary. Indeed, the situation may be the opposite of what most exegetes think: 'Gal 2.19 may contain the theological principle by which Paul interprets the ritual of baptism in Romans 6'.[1] That is, the theme of dying-and-rising with Christ, as it is outlined by Gal. 2.19, is more important in Paul's thought than is the theme of baptism. Since Gal. 2.20 is an echo and elaboration of 2.19, we are justified in saying the same of it.

In suggesting that dying-and-rising with Christ is more fundamental for Paul's soteriology than is baptism, Betz is in accord with the findings of this investigation. The aeon categories repeatedly noted above make re-enacting Christ's death and resurrection conceivable. They explain Paul's puzzling assertion in vv. 19-20 about somehow being dead and alive at the same time. For Paul, human existence occurs only within an aeon or sphere of power.[2] When believers die with Christ, they in effect die to the old aeon and are born (at least proleptically) to the new. The images of death and life convey the fact that an individual, upon entering a different sphere, becomes a different person.[3] Hence, Romans 5 makes at least as good a comparison with Gal. 2.19-20 as does Romans 6. Oepke realizes this when he says that one understands these verses best 'in the light of the Adam-Christ parallel (Rom. 5.12ff.; 1 Cor. 15.22, 45ff.). In the men of the first aeon lives the first Adam—in so far as one can speak here of life. However, in those who are transferred into the other aeon lives the second Adam, Christ, and this life is real life. Christ is the other aeon'![4]

---

1 Betz, *Galatians* 123.
2 Cf. *inter alia* Furnish, *Theology and Ethics* 115-18.
3 As Betz puts it, *Galatians* 123, 'For Paul, "crucifixion together with Christ" also means "crucifixion to the world" (6.14), and for that reason he can declare the "I" to be "dead" '.
4 Oepke, *Galater* 95. Cf. also J. Blank, *Paulus und Jesus* (StANT, 18; Munich: Kösel, 1968) 302.

Thus, the relative unimportance of Isaiah 53 and the importance of aeon categories have been demonstrated once more.

Philippians 2.6-11

Phil. 2.6-11, often called the Philippians hymn, is commonly judged to be non-Pauline.[1] Comparisons between it and the Suffering Servant Songs center around a similar overall structure (humiliation/exaltation)[2] and around certain terminological echoes. Among the latter, connections between Phil. 2.6, 7b and Isa. 52.14, 53.2 ('forms', *morphē*); between Phil. 2.7a and Isa. 53.12 ('emptied himself') and between Phil. 2.7b and Isa. 49.3, 5; 52.13; 53.11; 53.12 ('slave'[3], *doulos*), are most often mentioned.

The first of these presumed terminological connections is complicated by the fact that, for 'form', Isa. 52.14 LXX uses *eidos*, not *morphē*. Aquila, a second-century CE translator of the Old Testament into Greek, does employ *morphē* here, and it is argued that he represents an older text of Isaiah which Phil. 2.6-7 uses.[4] However, one is hard put to establish a definite link betweeen Aquila and Phil. 2.6-11.[5] Moreover, there remains in any event a significant difference between the meaning of 'form' in the Servant Songs and 'form' in the Philippians hymn. In the Songs it denotes the physical

---

1 Reasons for considering the hymn non-Pauline include: (1) vocabulary uncharacteristic of Paul; (2) the word 'who' in verse 6a, which customarily begins hymns; (3) a rhythmic structure suggestive of liturgical forms; and (4) a lack of the Pauline 'for us' or 'for you'. Many authors argue for non-Pauline authorship, e.g.: G. Bornkamm, 'On Understanding the Christ-Hymn', *Early Christian Experience* (New York and Evanston, Ill.: Harper, 1969) 112-13; Bultmann, *Theology* 129; J. Ernst, *Die Briefe an die Philipper, an Philemon, an die Kolosser, and die Epheser* (RNS, 7; part 3; Regensburg: Pustet, 1974) 65-66.

2 A. Feuillet, 'L'hymne christologique de l'épître aux Philippiens (II.6-11)', *RB* 72 (1965) 501; B. Reicke, 'Der Gottesknecht im Alten und Neuen Testament', *ThZ* 35 (1979) 349.

3 The Revised Standard Version unwisely uses 'servant' to translate *doulos* in Phil. 2.7b, but it does include 'slave' in a footnote.

4 K.F. Euler, *Die Verkündigung vom leidenden Gottesknecht aus Jes 53 in der griechischen Bibel* (Stuttgart & Berlin: Kohlhammer, 1934) 103; J.M. Furness, 'Behind the Philippian Hymn', *ExpT* 79 (1968) 181; Jeremias, *TDNT* 5.71n446.

5 L. Krinetzki, *Der Einfluss von Is LII, 13-LIII, 12 Par. auf Phil. II, 6-11* (Rome: Pontificum Athenaeum Anselmianum, 1959) 43.

appearance of the Servant, while in the hymn it characterizes modes of divine or human being. Even so avid a pursuer of parallels between the hymn and Isaiah as Krinetzki is reduced to calling the connections 'catchwords'.[1]

'Emptied himself' (Phil. 2.7a) has often been attributed to Isa. 53.12.[2] The phrase, it is said, is a direct translation of the Hebrew. Bornkamm has objected that the translation, if such it be, is not so close after all.[3] In addition, Phil. 2.7a talks of the incarnation, not of the crucifixion (as it would have to if it were being guided by Isa. 53.12).[4] However, Jeremias has responded to Bornkamm's doubts about the translation and maintains that the first two of the hymn's three four-line strophes are parallel, with each referring to the death.[5] Jeremias's response does seem possible, grammatically speaking.[6] But his claim that 'emptied himself' refers to the crucifixion has been little accepted.[7] Regardless of how the hymn is arranged, the fact that 'being born in the likeness of men' succeeds 'emptied himself' presents a problem for Jeremias's interpretation. To think of Christ as being crucified prior to assuming human form is difficult at best.

The term 'slave' (*doulos*; Phil. 2.7b) has been linked to a number of different passages in Isaiah,[8] There are three major theories in this regard. The first is that the hymn adverts to Isa. 52.13 MT.[9] According to this theory, the author of the hymn has simply chosen to translate the Hebrew into Greek with *doulos* instead of *pais* (the word for 'servant' which Isaiah 52–53 LXX uses and hence, the expected choice for any Greek translation of the Hebrew). The second theory is

1 Krinetzki, *Der Einfluss* 49.
2 E.g. C.H. Dodd, *According to the Scriptures* (Digswell Place, Great Britain: Nisbet, 1961) 93; C.H. Talbert, 'The Problem of Pre-Existence in Phil. 2.6-11', *JBL* 86 (1967) 152.
3 Bornkamm, 'On Understanding' 114-15; J. Gnilka, *Der Philipperbrief* (HThK, 10; fascicle 3; Freiburg, Basel & Vienna: Herder, 1968) 118.
4 Gnilka, *Philipperbrief* 118; H.-H. Schade, *Apokalyptische Christologie bei Paulus* (GTA 18; Göttingen: Vandenhoeck & Ruprecht, 1981) 65.
5 J. Jeremias, 'Zu Phil II 7: EKENΩΣEN 'EAYTON', *NovT* 6 (1963) 182-88.
6 *Contra* Deichgräber, *Gotteshymnus und Christushymnus* 123.
7 See n4 above.
8 Jeremias, *TDNT* 5.711; Krinetzki, *Der Einfluss* 34, 36.
9 Furness, 'Behind the Philippian Hymn' 181; Krinetzki, *Der Einfluss* 36; G. Stählin, 'ἴσος, κτλ.,' *TDNT* (1965) 353.

that, instead of *pais*, the hymn's author has utilized the *douleuonta* ('being a slave') of Isa. 53.11 LXX or the *doulon* ('slave'; accusative case) of Isa. 49.7 LXX. The author is supposed to have done this in order to offer a better contrast to the exalted Christ, who appears at the end of the hymn.[1] The third theory is that the hymn employs an unknown reading of Isaiah similar to Aquila or Symmachus (like Aquila, a second century CE translator of the Old Testament into Greek).[2] None of these theories is impossible, but their variety suggests the somewhat strained quality of attempts to get the hymn together with Isaiah at this point.

More conclusively, one can say that whatever the terminological links, the meanings of these two texts are quite distinct. The *pais* of Isa. 52.13 is primarily an honorific title, while in Phil. 2.7, *doulos* characterizes Christ's humiliation.[3] Moreover, *doulos* in Phil. 2.7b connotes human existence (as shown by its parallelism with 2.7c), something that can in no way be said of Isa. 52.13, 53.11, or 49.7.[4]

Lesser considerations against connecting Phil. 2.7 with the Servant include: (1) the lack of a definite article before *doulos* in Phil. 2.7;[5] (2) the differentiation from other people denoted by the Servant's activity, as opposed to the solidarity with humankind which Christ's servitude marks;[6] (3) the failure of Phil. 2.7 to read 'a slave of God', as it easily could have if a reference to Isaiah had been intended.[7]

Terminological echoes of Deutro-Isaiah have been claimed for a variety of the other words in the Philippian hymn. It is asserted that 'a thing to be grasped' (*harpagmos*; Phil. 2.6) may recall the *skula* ('spoils') of Isa. 49.24 LXX or the *laphura*

---

1 Krinetzki, *Der Einfluss* 37.

2 L. Cerfaux, *Christ in the Theology of St. Paul* (trans. G. Webb and A. Walker; Freiburg, Basel, & Vienna: Herder, 1959) 378n30; Talbert, 'The Problem of Pre-Existence' 152.

3 Hooker, *Jesus and the Servant* 120; Krinetzki, *Der Einfluss* 32-33.

4 Gnilka, *Philipperbrief* 120, 141.

5 Bornkamm, 'On Understanding' 114.

6 Bornkamm, 'On Understanding' 114; Schweizer, *Lordship* 63.

7 R.P. Martin, *Carmen Christi* (SNTSMS, 4; Cambridge: Cambridge University Press, 1967) 191.

('spoils') of Isa. 53.12 Aquila.[1] (*Laphura* is listed by Plutarch as a synonym for *harpagmos*.)[2]

This suggestion is, however, forced. The linguistic connection is indirect in both cases, and a glance at Isa. 53.12 shows the meaning of that verse to be quite different from the meaning of Phil. 2.6.

Also forced is the assertion that *homoioma* ('likeness') in Phil. 2.7c reflects *eidos* ('form') in Isa. 53.3 LXX. Paul is seen as refusing to use *eidos* here because it is his technical term for solidarity with humanity (cf. Rom. 8.3).[3] This ignores the probability that the hymn is non-Pauline. Furthermore, even if the hymn were Pauline, why would *eidos* be acceptable in Rom. 8.3—a very similar context—but not here?

Influence by Isa. 53.3 LXX is maintained with respect to the Greek word translated as 'men' in Phil. 2.7c.[4] But when Isaiah refers to the Servant as a 'man', it simply means to identify him as an individual or a person, while the hymn uses 'in the likeness of men' to characterize human existence *per se*.

The case is similar regarding the claim that *schema*, another Greek word translated as 'form' (Phil. 2.7d), has been used instead of the *eidos* of Isa. 53.3 LXX because a brief hymn needs a more pregnant term.[5] However, we are faced here not with a simple amplification, but with a genuine disparity of meaning. *Eidos*, in Isa. 53.3 LXX, points to an individual's appearance; *schema*, in Phil. 2.7d, to the structure of a mode of being.

'Humbled himself' (Phil. 2.8a) has been traced to Isa. 53.4,[6] 53.7,[7] and 53.8.[8] Once more, however, there is a distinct difference between the hymn and its alleged counterparts. Christ humbles himself deliberately and in obedience, while the

---

1 Furness, 'Behind the Philippian Hymn' 181.
2 Plutarch, *de Alex.* i, 8.
3 Krinetzki, *Der Einfluss* 49-50, 52n127.
4 Krinetzki, *Der Einfluss* 51
5 Krientzki, *Der Einfluss* 51.
6 Jeremias suggests a comparison with Isa. 53.4 Hexapla, *TDNT* 5.709n446. Krinetzki refutes this, *Der Einfluss* 54-55.
7 Krinetzki, *Der Einfluss* 55; Talbert, 'The Problem of Pre-Existence' 152.
8 Cerfaux, *Christ* 390.

enemies forcibly humble the Servant.[1] No statement of obedience is made concerning the Servant in his humiliation.

'Obedient' (Phil. 2.8) is considered to reflect three Isaianic passages: Isa. 50.4-5 MT/LXX,[2] 53.7,[3] and 53.10.[4] The first of these passages is highly problematical, despite claims that the Greek verb for 'hear' (Isa. 50.4b LXX) is etymologically related to the word for 'obedient' in Phil. 2.8 and that the phrase 'I was not rebellious' of Isa. 50.5a LXX is similar in meaning to 'become obedient'.[5] The second passage has difficulties, too, since the thought of obedience which is supposed to form the link must be introduced into Isa. 53.7; all that the latter really speaks of is the Servant's mute endurance.[6] Isa. 53.10 enters the picture as a kind of adjunct to 53.7. Its comments on Yahweh make clear, it is said, that 53.7 is actually describing the Servant's obedience.[7] This is incorrect, however. If anything, 53.10 removes the issue of obedience even further from consideration, since it leaves virtually no room for the Servant's own violation.[8]

'Unto death' (Phil. 2.8) has been connected with Isa. 53.7 LXX,[9] 53.8 LXX,[10] and 53.12 LXX.[11] But there is no particular reason why an author referring to the first and/or third of these should not use their Greek for 'unto death' instead of the different Greek found in the hymn. Nor can one overlook the fact that again there is no indication in the Isaianic texts of the obedience so important in the hymn. Christ's death is the nat-

---

1 Krinetzki, *Der Einfluss* 54-55, O. Michel, 'Zur Exegese von Phil 2.5-11', *Theologie als Glaubenswagnis* (Hamburg: Furche-Verlag, 1954) 88-89.

2 Krinetzki, *Der Einfluss* 65–65.

3 Krinetzki, *Der Einfluss* 59–61.

4 Krinetzki, *Der Einfluss* 63.

5 Krinetzki, *Der Einfluss* 64–65.

6 Cf. Krinetzki, *Der Einfluss* 60.

7 Krinetzki, *Der Einfluss* 63.

8 E. Larson, *Christus als Vorbild* (Acta seminarii Neotestamentici Upsaliensis 23; Lund: Gleerup, 1962) 250-51, states that the decisive evidence for the relation of the hymn to Isa. 53 is the stress of both on obedience. But this statement is supported, oddly, by reference to an Adam typology and Rom. 5.19-21. Larsson offers no real evidence for his assertion.

9 Krinetzki, *Der Einfluss* 66.

10 Davies, *Paul and Rabbinic Judaism* 274; Furness, 'Behind the Philippian Hymn' 181.

11 Cerfaux, *Christ* 392; Krinetzki, *Der Einfluss* 66.

ural and ultimate extension of his obedience. Nothing of the sort is said regarding the Servant.

Krinetzki's suggestion that 'cross' (Phil. 2.8) refers to Isa. 53.5 MT is forced.[1]

'Therefore' (Phil 2.9a) reflects, it is said, Isa. 53.12 LXX,[2] Isa. 53.23 MT,[3] or both.[4] This is conceivable, but several complications remain. First, and with regard to the Septuagint, it must be asked why its Greek for 'therefore' would have been changed to what is found in the hymn. Secondly, and in general, there is the issue of different sequences: in Isaiah, 'therefore' follows the exaltation, but in the hymn, it immediately precedes the exaltation. Hence, one must conclude that if a connection is present here, it can be only a relatively distant one.

The 'exalted' of Phil. 2.9 has been linked to the 'exalted' of Isa. 52.13 LXX,[5] although Jeremias insists on the Masoretic text.[6] Again there is a lack of full correspondence between the terms used, since the Greek verb in the Septuagint is the superlative of that in Phil. 2.9. Most commentators pass over this fact, but Cerfaux asserts that Paul uses the superlative because he wants to show Christ raised above the cosmic powers.[7] Krinetzki believes that the use of superlatives is an 'attribute of the Pauline prison letters'.[8] Both of these explanations are, however, speculative.

When we arrive at Phil. 2.10-11, we find that this passage does appear to have transmogrified Isa. 45.23 by employing the notion of cosmic powers.[9] But this remains cold comfort for advocates of a link between the Philippians hymn and the

---

1 Krinetzki, *Der Einfluss* 68.

2 Cerfaux, *Christ* 379n37; D.M. Stanley, 'The Theme of the Servant of Yahweh in Primitive Christian Soteriology and its Transposition by St. Paul', *CBQ* 16 (1954) 422.

3 Jeremias, *TDNT* 5.712n446.

4 Krinetzki, *Der Einfluss* 69.

5 L.L. Carpenter, *Primitive Christian Application of the Doctrine of the Servant* (Durham, N.C.: Duke University Press, 1929) 78; Euler, *Die Verkündigung* 47, 100-1.

6 Jeremias, *TDNT* 5.712n446.

7 Cerfaux, *Christ* 379n37.

8 Krinetzki, *Der Einfluss* 72.

9 Bornkamm, 'On Understanding' 116; Bultmann, *Theology* 2.153; G.B. Caird, *Principalities and Powers* (Oxford: Clarendon, 1956) 97.

Suffering Servant Songs of Isaiah 52–53. Here the hymn has taken a passage which is not even part of the Songs and then given it a substantially new cast. The pattern of thought is from 'the world of religious Hellenism',[1] in which cosmic powers exercise influence over people and must be placated or vanquished.

This reference to the powers, plus the notion of a divine figure who assumes human form and then reassumes divine form, places the hymn in a radically different thought-world from that occupied by the Servant Songs. The hymn characterizes human existence as servitude (2.7), apparently under the sway of the cosmic powers,[2] above whom Christ is set (2.10-11), because (2.9) of his obedience unto death (2.8). Here, as before, we find two spheres or dominions, with Jesus' death as the turning point after which the benevolent dominion (with Christ as lord) gains control over the malevolent one.

This pattern, as mentioned, separates the hymn sharply from the Servant Songs. The terminological echoes examined above may indeed be genuine, but this gap in meaning cannot be overcome by what are at most catchwords.[3]

We have seen, then, five reasons why a formative impact of the songs on the hymn is unlikely: (1) the lack of exact correspondence of language; (2) the lack of sequential correspondence;[4] (3) the switching that must be assumed between the Septuagint and Masoretic text;[5] (4) the failure of the songs to parallel the central position given to obedience by the hymn;[6] and (5) the overall conceptual gap between the Songs and the hymn. To these five reasons two more may now be added: the failure of the hymn to develop any of the seemingly

---

1 D. Georgi, 'Der vorpaulinische Hymnus Phil 2.6-11', *Zeit und Geschichte* (ed. E. Dinkler; Tübingen: Mohr, 1964) 264.

2 Käsemann, 'Critical Analysis of Philippians 2.5-11', trans. A.F. Carse, ed. R.W. Funk, *Journal for Theology and the Church* 5 (1968) 67.

3 See above, p. 51n1.

4 Martin, *Carmen Christi* 186.

5 G. Strecker, 'Redaktion und Tradition im Christushymnus Phil 2.6-11' *ZNW* 55 (1964) 73; Wengst, *Christologische Formeln* 146.

6 Cf. S.K. Williams, *Jesus' Death* 49.

fertile soteriological material in the Songs,[1] and the absence of any hint of pre-existence in the latter.[2]

It remains to be said that Paul has given no indication in his remarks surrounding the hymn that the Servant is a consideration for him here. Käsemann's criticism of a simplistic, ethical interpretation of Phil. 2.6-11 is valid,[3] but it should not blind one to the parenetic aspects of the hymn's setting. The hymn itself is clearly concerned with the mythic career of Christ rather than with ethics, but this does not prevent Paul from employing it parenetically. Be minded towards each other as you are 'in Christ', he tells the Philippians.[4] Later, he seems to pick up the motif of Jesus' obedience and recommend the same quality to his audience.[5] A few verses after that (Phil. 2.14), his allusion to the citizens of the old and new aeons recalls the hymn's distinction between the rule of the powers and that of Christ. These two features, then, appear to be the most important for Paul with regard to the hymn: obedience and the two opposing spiritual realms. As distant as any reference to the Servant may be from the hymn, it is even further from Paul himself.

Conclusion

This chapter has demonstrated that Paul makes no fundamental use of the Suffering Servant in his soteriology. Those passages which various authors have labeled references to the Servant have proven to be either dubious or isolated. As in Chapter 1, we have found that the basis of Paul's soteriology is Jesus' obedient death as the turning point of the aeons.

1 Martin, *Carmen Christi* 317; D.M. Stanley, *Christ's Resurrection in Pauline Soteriology* (AnBib, 13; Rome: Pontifical Biblical Institute, 1961) 101-2.
2 R. Schnackenburg, 'Christologie des Neuen Testaments' in *Das Christusereignis*, vol. 3, part 1 of *Mysterium Salutis. Grundriss Heilsgeschichtlicher Dogmatik* (ed. J. Feiner and M. Löhrer; Einsiedeln, Zurich, and Cologne: Benziger 1970) 322.
3 Käsemann, 'Critical Analysis' 83-84.
4 Käsemann, 'Critical Analysis' 84.
5 This does not vitiate Käsemann's argument. One should, however, point out that the sphere of power called 'in Christ' was established by Christ's deeds; the line between the two cannot be absolute. Cf. M.D. Hooker, 'Phil. 2.6-11', *Jesus und Paulus* (eds. E.E. Ellis and E. Grässer; Göttingen: Vandenhoeck & Ruprecht, 1975) 152-57.

Chapter 3

PAUL'S DOCTRINE OF SALVATION AND THE BINDING OF ISAAC (GENESIS 22)

Introduction

This chapter will investigate the extent to which the Akedah or 'binding' of Isaac may have been significant in Paul's formulation of his soteriology. There is currently some debate over the definition of the term 'Akedah'. P.R. Davies and B.D. Chilton have defined it as 'a haggadic presentation of the vicariously atoning sacrifice of Isaac in which he is said, e.g. 'to have shed his blood freely and/or to have been reduced to ashes'.[1] This definition has an obvious utility in determining Christian backgrounds, since it specifies a saving signifiance for Isaac's death in terms of vicariousness and atonement. However, it has been criticized as being too narrow by Hayward[2] and Swetnam.[3] Because of this controversy the term will be avoided here. Instead, reference will be made simply to Genesis 22, and the interpretation attached to it (e.g. vicarious, non-vicarious) will be explicated as need be.

Romans 3.24-25

Some authors have proposed that these verses refer to Genesis 22. Specifically, it is maintained that the Greek translated by 'put forward' in Rom. 3.25 is itself a translation of the Hebrew behind 'provide' in Gen. 22.8.[4] However, this suggestion has received no support because the Septuagint does not use the

---

1 P.R. Davies and B.D. Chilton, 'The Aqedah: A Revised Tradition History', *CBQ* 40 (1978) 515.
2 R. Hayward, 'The Present State of Research into the Targumic Account of the Sacrifice of Isaac', *JJS* 32 (1981) 129.
3 J. Swetnam, *Jesus and Isaac* (AnBib, 94; Rome: Biblical Institute, 1981) 18.
4 G. Klein, *Studien über Paulus* (Stockholm: Bonniers, 1918); Schoeps, *Paul* 146; idem, 'The Sacrifice of Isaac in Paul's Theology', *JBL* 65 (1946) 390.

Greek verb for 'put forward' in Rom. 3.25 to translate the Hebrew verb for 'provide' in Gen. 22.8.[1]

Romans 4.25

Several writers have argued that this verse constitutes a reference to a vicarious, sacrificial death on the part of Isaac.[2] Others, however, have noted that 4.25 refers *not* to Genesis 22 but to Genesis 15 and 17.[3] As Barrett puts it, for Paul, 'the outstanding example of Abraham's faith was not his willingness to sacrifice his son but his confident belief that God would give him and his wife a child, notwithstanding their great age'.[4]

Romans 5.9

Schoeps[5] and Hillyer[6] argue that here Paul is referring to the Passover and subsequently to the vicarious, sacrificial death of Isaac. This link is accomplished via an interpretation of the Passover (found in the rabbinic text Mekhilta 8a) which ascribes its saving power to Isaac's death. This seems eisegetical. There is no evidence that Paul had the Passover or Genesis 22 in mind while writing this verse. Also, there are serious difficulties with the dating of the Mekhilta.[7]

Schoeps[8] and Hillyer[9] also argue that Paul was aware of a tradition according to which Isaac's trial took place on a Passover. However, the attestation of this 'tradition' is problem-

---

1 L.E. Wood, 'Isaac Typology in the New Testament', *NTS* 14 (1967-68) 587.
2 N. Hillyer, 'The Servant of God', *EvQ* 41 (1969) 152; Schoeps, *Paul* 146; *idem*, 'The Sacrifice of Isaac' 65, 390.
3 Barrett, *Romans* 29; Davies-Chilton, 'The Aqedah' 532; R. Le Déaut, *La Nuit Pascale* (AnBib, 22; Rome: Institut Biblique Pontifical, 1963) 205, writes that the reference is to Gen. 15.6.
4 Barrett, *Romans* 29.
5 Schoeps, *Paul* 147; *idem*, 'The Sacrifice of Isaac' 391.
6 Hillyer, 'The Servant of God' 152.
7 Cf. B.Z. Wacholder's assertion that the Mekhilta has an 8th-century date: 'The date of the Mekilta de-Rabbi Ishmael', *HUCA* 39 (1968) 117-44; cf. also Davies-Chilton, 'The Aqedah' 53n57; M. Smith, 'On the Problem of Method in the Study of Rabbinic Literature', *JBL* 92 (1973) 112-14; B.Z. Wacholder, 'A Reply', *JBL* 92 (1973) 114-15.
8 Schoeps, *Paul* 147; *idem*, 'The Sacrifice' 391.
9 Hillyer, 'The Servant of God' 152.

atical[1] and, in any case, there is no reference at 5.9 to the Passover.

Romans 8.32

Commentators agree that this verse is the strongest candidate for a link between Genesis 22 and the Pauline interpretation of Jesus' saving death. Rom. 8.32a contains the phrase 'did not spare his own son'. This is compared to Gen. 22.12 and 16 LXX,

---

1 This 'tradition' is allegedly reflected in the Book of Jubilees, and in the rabbinic writings of the Midrashim and the Targumim. Davies and Chilton have subjected the first to a rigorous critique on this count. To begin with, Jubilees' connection between Isaac and the Passover is only implicit. Jubilees 17.15 states that 'in the seventh week, in the first year thereof, in the first month in this jubilee, on the twelfth of this month', heavenly voices were singing Abraham's praises (translation from R.H. Charles, ed., *The Apocrypha and Pseudepigrapha of the Old Testament* [2 vols.; Oxford: Oxford University Press, 1913] 2.39). In response, the evil Mastema challenged God to demand the sacrifice of Isaac as a test. God did so, Abraham journeyed toward the place of sacrifice, and 'on the third day saw his destination' (18.4). This puts the sacrifice on the 15th Nisan. While the dating is suggestive, the fact remains that nothing explicit is made of any connection between Isaac and the Passover (cf. Davies–Chilton, 'The Aqedah' 519).

Moreover, one must allow for Jubilees' practice of tying all major events in the lives of the patriarchs to Jewish festivals. Not only is Isaac's sacrifice placed on Passover, but so are the building of Noah's Ark, Abraham's sacrifice at Shechem, and Jacob's dream. Must all of these correspondences be taken as indicating developed doctrines?

Davies and Chilton also reject the assumption that, since Jubilees mentions Moriah and Zion, Issac is to be linked with the Passover lambs. What they call a 'piece of pious geography' is found also in Chronicles, where it clearly has no such implication. Therefore, 'why should it here?' (519). It is important that Isaac's sacrifice may be seen here as prefiguring the Temple cult, but this does not point to Passover (519).

The dating of Midrashic and Targumic literature is notoriously imprecise. J.C. Greenfield, review of J.W. Etheridge, *The Targums of Onkelos and Jonathan ben Uzziel on the Pentateuch, with the Fragments of the Jerusalem Targum from the Chaldee*, JBL 89 (1970) 238-39, denies the antiquity of the Targumim. J. Fitzmyer, 'The Languages of First Century Palestine', CBQ 32 (1970) 532, places them after 200 CE. See also *idem*, review of M. McNamara, *The New Testament and the Palestinian Targum to the Pentateuch*, TS 29 (1968) 322-26; *idem*, review of A.D. Macho, *Neophyti 1*, CBQ 32 (1970) 106-13. B.Z. Wacholder, review of M. McNamara, *Targum and Testament*, JBL 93 (1974) 132-33, states that the Palestinian Targumim cannot be dated before the ninth or tenth centuries. E.P. Sanders is 'not persuaded of the antiquity of the Targums as we have them', and maintains that, for the most part, 'the present state of Targumic studies does not permit the Targums to be used' in New Testament scholarship, *Paul and Palestinian Judaism* 25-26.

both of which address Abraham's failure to spare his son.[1] However, this comparison has been questioned, either because so little of the Greek is identical,[2] because of the awkwardness of judging God's actions by those of Abraham,[3] or because of the paucity of Paul's explicit references to Genesis 22 (even in Rom. 4).[4]

Others object that, while there may be an allusion to Genesis 22 here, it can hardly be said that Rom. 8.32 demonstrates a role for that chapter in Pauline soteriology. This is because the verse is directed not towards the victims (Isaac–Jesus), but towards those who gave the victims up (Abraham–God).[5]

This last objection does indeed seem to be definitive. The question which 8.32 answers is asked in 8.31b: 'If God is for us, who is against us'? Rom. 8.32 is concerned not with an Isaac typology, but with the trustworthiness of God. When it does refer to the saving significance of Jesus' death, its language suggests, if anything, Isaiah 53. Nor does the context indicate any influence by Genesis 22.[6] As seen above, Rom. 8.32 stands in a strongly apocalyptic section. There is, finally, nothing here that suggests Paul is modeling his interpretation of Jesus' saving death on that of Isaac. At most, it can be said that, through a brief allusion to Genesis 22, he is stressing the devotedness of God to his people.

---

1   The following authors, *inter alia*, assert that Rom. 8.32 refers to Genesis 22: Cerfaux, *Christ* 125; N. Dahl, 'The Atonement—An Adequate Reward for the Akedah? (Rom. 8.32)', *Neotestamentica et Semitica* (ed. E.E. Ellis and M. Wilcox; Edinburgh: Clark, 1969) 15; M. Wilcox, ' "Upon the Tree"—Deut. 21, 22-23 in the New Testament', *JBL* 96 (1977) 98.

2   Kramer, *Christ* 27n404.

3   Schlier, *Römerbrief* 277.

4   H. Paulsen, *Überlieferung und Auslegung in Römer 8* (WMANT, 8; Neukirchen-Vluyn: Neukirchener, 1974) 167; H. von Reventlow, *Opfere deinen Sohn* (BS, 53; Neukirchen-Vluyn: Neukirchener, 1968) 79-80.

5   P.R. Davies, 'Passover and the Dating of the Aqedah', *JJS* 30 (1979) 66; Davies–Chilton, 'The Aqedah' 530; Wilckens, *Römer* 2.173n772.

6   Paulsen, *Überlieferung* 167. Swetnam, *Jesus and Isaac* 81, claims that the lack of any reference in the context to Genesis 22 shows the widespread popularity of the Isaac-Christ typology and the familiarity of Paul's readers with it. Such an argument from silence is inherently weak, however, especially in light of the paucity of allusions elsewhere in early Christian literature.

1 Corinthians 5.7

Schoeps[1] and Hillyer[2] consider this verse a reference to Genesis 22 for the same reasons that pertained in the case of Rom. 5.9.[3] However, the evidence linking Passover to Genesis 22 has just been examined, and in the absence of any indication that Paul does have Genesis 22 in mind here, the claim must be regarded as unlikely.

1 Corinthians 11.25-26

The attempt (referred to in the previous two segments) to link a vicarious, sacrifical death of Isaac to Passover arises in Vermes' treatment of these verses.[4] Yet it has been noted that links between the Passover and Genesis 22 cannot be adequately demonstrated for this period. Furthermore, Vermes' assertions rest on the basis of an 'Akedah theology' he believes he has reconstructed.[5] But the intertestamental literature which he employs to date his reconstruction does not support his conclusions.[6]

1 Corinthians 15.4

R. Daly maintains that K. Lehmann's study has shown this verse to be 'a highly probable allusion to the Akedah'.[7] But in fact Lehmann's work does not warrant such a claim It traces what Lehmann believes to be a rich tradition of 'the third day' through the rabbinic literature of the Midrashim and Targumim. The tradition includes references to Genesis 22, but does not depend on that text alone. It is more accurate to say that Lehmann sets 1 Cor. 15.4 in this overall context than to say that he orients it towards Genesis 22 in particular.[8]

1 Schoeps, *Paul* 147; *idem*, 'The Sacrifice' 391.
2 Hillyer, 'The Servant of God' 152.
3 See above, p. 60.
4 G. Vermes, 'Redemption and Genesis xxii—The Binding of Isaac and the Sacrifice of Jesus', *Scripture and Tradition in Judaism* (SPB 4; 2nd edn; Leiden: E.J. Brill, 1973) 226.
5 Vermes, 'Redemption' 226.
6 Cf. Davies–Chilton, 'The Aqedah' 55-63.
7 Daly, 'The Soteriological Significance' 71.
8 Lehmann, *Auferweckt* 280.

Despite claiming Lehmann's work as an indication that 1 Cor. 15.4 points specifically to Gensis 22, Daly seems aware of the broad tradition for which Lehmann argues. He acknowledges that 'on the third day' refers in a general fashion to the 'start of a new time of blessing or salvation'.[1] Similarly, in his conclusion, he retreats somewhat from his earlier stance by saying that the phrase 'cannot but *include* an allusion to the Akedah'[2] (italics mine). Yet it is entirely conceivable that 'on the third day' includes an allusion to Genesis 22 only in the sense that the 'forty days' of Mk 1.13 includes an allusion to Noah's sojourn on the floodwaters. In both cases, a clichéd number is used with no necessary connection to any one of many possible allusions. Moreover, if a single Old Testament passage is indeed at issue here, it is most likely Hos. 6.2-3.[3]

Finally, there is the problem of dating. Attributing an early date to Midrashic and Targumic literature is difficult if not impossible. Thus, Conzelmann dismisses Lehmann's thesis with a terse 'But the evidence is late'.[4]

Galatians 1.4

Schoeps[5] and Wood[6] assert that this verse is a parallel to Genesis 22. There is little or no reason to say this, however.[7] Gal. 1.4 seems clearly indebted to an aeon-conceptuality.

Galatians 3.13-14

Dahl argues that 3.14a paraphrases Gen. 22.18 (though he says 'the blessing of Abraham' comes from Gen. 28.4).[8] He also believes that the substitutionary theme of 3.13 relates to Genesis 22. The manner of this relation is rather complicated. Dt. 21.23 states that a man who is hanged is cursed. To evade this possible charge against Jesus' Messiahship, the 'ram

1 Daly, 'The Soteriological Significance' 71.
2 Daly, 'The Soteriological Significance' 71.
3 Cf., however, Lehmann, *Auferweckt* 225-30.
4 Conzelmann, *Corinthians* 256n68.
5 Schoeps, *Paul* 146; *idem*, 'The Sacrifice' 390.
6 Wood, 'The Servant' 153.
7 Barrett, *Romans* 29.
8 Dahl, 'The Atonement' 23.

caught in a thicket' of Gen. 22.13 is brought in. Jesus is thus seen as the sacrificial creature which God provides. Dahl admits, however, that this typology equates Jesus and the ram rather than Jesus and Isaac.

Vermes maintains that in both 3.13 and 3.14 Paul 'obviously has Genesis xxii. 18 in mind',[1] but does not elaborate.

Daly states that Gal. 3.13-14 'seems to be a fairly clear allusion to the sacrifice of Isaac'.[2] He also states that it 'would appear to be adequately explainable merely by reference to the OT (Gen. 22.18 and 28.4)',[3] references which, to his mind, do *not* involve the sacrifice of Isaac. The apparent contradiction is not resolved.

Finally, it should be noted that Le Déaut considers a Jesus-Isaac typology as 'sous-jacente' in Galatians 3, but not as referred to explicitly.[4]

This list of advocates for a connection between 3.13-14 and Genesis 22 shows that even those who take such a position are relatively tentative. No one argues straightforwardly that the passage in Galatians reflects a vicarious, sacrificial death on the part of Isaac. Dahl opts instead for a strained comparison with the ram,[5] Vermes leaves his claim unclarified, Daly apparently discounts any reference to a sacrifice of Isaac,[6] and Le Déaut holds the typology to be no more than implicit.[7]

Added to these considerations is the fact that Betz believes the textual reference for the 'blessing of Abraham' cannot be precisely determined in the first place.[8]

It is probable that this passage should be interpreted as Betz does, in terms of the aeon conceptuality evident in 4.3-6. The 'curse of the Torah' is thus identified with 'the elements of the

---

1 Vermes, 'Redemption' 220.
2 Daly, 'The Soteriological Significance' 72.
3 Daly, 'The Soteriological Significance' 72.
4 Le Déaut, *La Nuit Pascale* 202n185.
5 Dahl, 'The Atonement' 23.
6 Daly, 'The Soteriological Significance' 72.
7 Le Déaut, *La Nuit Pascale* 202-203.
8 Betz, *Galatians* 142n32.

world'. Entering and inhabiting this old aeon, Christ gains freedom for those who are enslaved by it.[1]

1 Thessalonians 5.10

Schoeps compares this verse to Genesis 22,[2] but this is hardly likely, since there is no indication in the text for it.[3] Rather, the references to wrath in 5.9, to day/light vs. night/darkness in 5.5, and to military readiness in 5.8 suggest aeon conceptuality.[4]

Conclusion

This survey of purported allusions to Genesis 22 shows that there is no basis for the claim that Paul has used its story about Isaac to structure his own soteriology. As in the first two chapters, aeon-categories have instead come to the fore as the means by which Paul expresses the significance of Jesus' death.

---

1 Betz, *Galatians* 149-50. For the relationship between 3.13-14 and 4.3-6, cf. R.B. Hays, *The Faith of Jesus Christ* (SBLDS, 56; Chico, CA: Scholars Press, 1983) 85-104.

2 Schoeps, *Paul* 146.

3 Barrett, *Romans* 28.

4 E. Lövestam, *Spiritual Wakefulness in the New Testament* (Lunds Universitets Arsskrift; N.F. Avd. 1, vol. 55; no. 3; Lund: Gleerup, 1963) 27, 51; A. Oepke, 'ὅπλον', *TDNT* 5 (1967) 294; E.P. Sanders, *Paul and Palestinian Judaism* 465, 511.

Chapter 4

PAUL'S DOCTRINE OF SALVATION
AND THE MYSTERY RELIGIONS
(ATTIS, ADONIS, ISIS, OSIRIS, ELEUSIS)

Introduction

It has often been alleged that Paul's concept of baptism as dying and rising with Christ shows the influence of Mystery religions.[1] The difficulty with this allegation lies in finding examples of Mysteries in which the initiate dies and rises—or at least dies—with the cult deity. This fact will become evident from the following survey of the relevant Mysteries.

The survey will also look at the issue of cultic meals, the second alleged point of contact between Paul and the Mysteries.[2]

The procedure here will be sequential, examining in turn each of the major Mystery deities.[3]

---

1 Cf. the authors discussed by G. **Wagner**, *Pauline Baptism and the Pagan Mysteries* (trans. J.P. Smith; Edinburgh & London: Oliver & Boyd, 1967) 7-47. Cf. also the literature cited by Friedrich, *Die Verkündigung* 87-89, and by D.H. Wiens, 'Mystery Concepts in Primitive Christianity and its Environment', *ANRW* II/23.2 (1980) 1253-55.

2 For literature and analysis, cf. Klauck, *Herrenmahl passim*, and W.L. Willis, *Idol Meat in Corinth* (SBLDS, 68; Chico, CA: Scholars Press, 1985). Cf. also J.P. Kane, 'The Mithraic cult meal in its Greek and Roman environment', *Mithraic Studies* II (ed. J.R. Hinnells; Manchester: Manchester University Press, 1975) 313-51.

3 I do not deal here with Mithras, because of the lateness of the popularity of his cult and because he does not die.

    I do not deal with Tammuz-Dumuzi because of the improbability of a Hellenistic Jew like Paul being influenced by a native, Syrian cult.

    I do not deal with Dionysus because there is little or no solid evidence for a ritualistic dying-and-rising with him, despite some scholars' attempted reconstructions of the Dionysiac cult. Cf. P. McGinty, *Interpretation and Dionysos* (RR, 16; The Hague, Paris, & New York: Morton, 1978) chs. 2, 3 and 5. In the classical period, the myth of a dismembered and reanimated Dionysus is testified by 'only a few very *oblique* and uncertain references', N.J. Richardson, 'Early Greek views about life after death', *Greek Religion and Society* (ed. P.E. Easterling and J.V. Muir; Cambridge: Cambridge University Press, 1985) 62. Cf. also W. Burkert,

Attis

Baptism into Attis

There is no evidence that baptismal rites played a role in Attis-worship.

Attis' Death

It is not Attis' death, but his castration, which becomes the central motif in later versions of the myth.[1] That the centrality of this motif could push out even the mention of Attis' death is shown by Catullus,[2] Julian,[3] Lucian,[4] Minucius Felix,[5] Ovid,[6] and Sallustius.[7] All of these writers provide substantial accounts of Attis' story with no reference to his death. In the versions they cite, the important thing was that he castrated himself. It is possible, of course, that the authors named above were aware of versions which included Attis' death. But if so, they did not consider these versions significant enough to report.

Greek Religion (trans. J. Raffan; Cambridge, MA: Harvard University Press, 1985) 294, who writes: 'Our knowledge of the [Bacchic] rites, myths, and doctrines, remains, of course, very fragmentary'.

Matters are not much clearer for the Hellenistic-Roman period. M.P. Nilsson finds no reason to interpret the Bacchic Mysteries of the time as containing a dying-and-rising with the deity, 'The Bacchic Mysteries of the Roman Age', *HTS* 46 (1953) 184. Cf. also Nilsson's doubts about the Dionysiac myth, *The Dionysiac Mysteries of the Hellenistic and Roman Age* (Skrifter Utgivna av Svenska Institutet I Athen 8; Lund: Gleerup, 1957) 111.

Ovid ignores the issue of Dionysus' death, *Metamorphoses* 3.314. Plutarch seems to regard the Dionysiac rites as important for the knowledge they convey, not for any change which they objectively effect in the life of the initiate, *Moralia* 996 B-C. This agrees with S.G. Cole's findings, 'New Evidence for the Mysteries of Dionysos', *GRBS* 21 (1980) 233-34.

1   M.P. Nilsson, *Geschichte der griechischen Religion* (2nd edn; Munich: Beck, 1955-57) 2.643; cf. also Wagner, *Baptism* 215-16, and C. Colpe, 'Zur mythologischen Struktur der Adonis-, Attis- und Osiris-Überlieferungen', *lišan mithurti* (AOAT 1; in cooperation with M. Dietrich; ed. W. Rollig; Kevelaer: Butzon & Bercker; Neukirchen-Vluyn: Neukirchener Verlag, 1969) 37. See also W. Burkert, *Structure and History in Greek Mythology and Ritual* (SCS, 47; Berkeley: University of California Press, 1979) 104.

2   Catullus 63.

3   Julian, *Orations* V.167C-169D.

4   Lucian, *De Dea Syria* 50-51.

5   Minucius Felix, *Octavius* 22.4

6   Ovid, *Fasti* 4.221-46.

7   Sallustius, *De diis et mundo* 4.

The Attis-myth of Paul's day, therefore, possessed no uniform focus on its protagonist's death. This fact does not preclude the possibility of Paul having had contact with versions in which Attis' death played a part. It does, however, make speculation about such contact that much more difficult.

Attis' Resurrection

Except for Firmicus Maternus,[1] all the authors who do mention Attis' death omit any reference to a resurrection.[2] Nilsson and Wagner suggest that Firmicus' attachment of Attis to the cycle of planting and harvesting betrays Eleusinian influence.[3] It is also possible, of course, that a fourth-century Christian such as he would have interpreted the Attis-myth in Christian terms (even while polemicizing against it). In any case, Firmicus' claim of a resurrection stands alone among the sources.[4]

Dying and Rising with Attis

There is no evidence that the death of Attis (or, with regard to Firmicus, his resurrection) was viewed as a participatory event.[5] The rituals known as the *Hilaria* were oriented toward Cybele, not Attis, and they seem to have constituted a simple festival rather than the celebration of a resurrection.[6] According to Nilsson, the whole matter may have been just an expression of the polarities of life.[7] Neither can the Tauro-

---

1 Firmicus Maternus, *De errore* 3.1. H. Hepding, *Attis, seine Mythen und sein Kult* (RVV 1; Giessen: Töpelmann, 1903) 197, believes that *De errore* 22.1 refers to Attis, but as noted below, it actually concerns Osiris.

2 Nilsson, *Geschichte* 2.649-51; Wagner, *Baptism* 217-20. Cf. also Burkert, *Structure and History* 101; Colpe, 'Zur mythologischen' 42-43; Klauck, *Herrenmahl* 119n190; B.M. Metzger, 'Methodology in the Study of the Mystery Religions and Early Christianity', *Historical and Literary Studies* (NTTS, 8; Grand Rapids, Mich.: Eerdmans, 1968) 20; R.H. Nash, *Christianity and the Hellenistic World* (Grand Rapids, Mich.: Zondervan; Dallas: Probe Ministries International, 1984) 172; A. Oepke, 'ἐγείρω', *TDNT* 2 (1964) 336.

3 Nilsson, *Geschichte* 2.650; Wagner, *Baptism* 220.

4 E. Lohse, *The New Testament Environment* (trans. J.E. Steely; Nashville: Abingdon, 1976) 240, asserts the reawakening of Attis, but does not refer to any source.

5 Wagner, *Baptism* 220-54.

6 Nilsson, *Geschichte* 2.650-51; Wagner, *Baptism* 225-29.

7 Nilsson, *Geschichte* 2.650.

boleum be adduced as evidence for dying and rising with Attis. Interpreting the descent into the pit as a death experience is not warranted by the evidence.[1] References to the participant in this rite as being reborn appear only in late texts.[2] Although an inscription from 376 AD states that the participant is reborn in eternity,[3] earlier testimonies indicate that 28 years was the period of re-birth.[4] This does not conform with the thesis that the re-birth of an immortal god is being shared. There is no ground for concluding that Attis somehow conferred immortality.[5]

It may be said that the fate of Attis is imitated by his and Cybele's devotees (the *Galloi*) when they castrate themselves. But this imitation seems motivated more by a desire for complete devotion to the Goddess than a concern with Attis himself.[6] At any rate, this ritual can scarcely be regarded as dying and rising with Attis.

Attis' Cult Meal

Nearly the sole evidence for any sort of meal in the Attis cult consists of two citations from Clement of Alexandria and Firmicus Maternus. The former quotes followers of Cybele and Attis as saying: 'I ate from the drum [*tympanos*]; I drank from

---

1 Wagner, *Baptism* 252.
2 A.D. Nock, 'Early Gentile Christianity and its Hellenistic Background', *Essays on Religion and the Ancient World* (ed. Z. Stewart; 2 vols.; Cambridge, MA: Harvard University Press, 1972) 1.103; G. Showerman, *The Great Mother of the Gods* (Madison, Wis.: University of Wisconsin Press, 1901) 280; Wagner, *Baptism* 253.
3 Hepding, *Attis* 89n37. The phrase may in fact echo Christianity. Cf. R. Duthoy, *The Tauroboleum: Its Evolution and Terminology* (Leiden: Brill, 1969) 119-21; H. Graillot, *Le culte de Cybèle, mère des dieux, à Rome et dans l'Empire romain* (Bibliothèque des Écoles françaises d'Athènes et de Rome 107; Paris: Fontemoing, 1912) 171; H. Rahner, 'Das christliche Mysterium und die heidnischen Mysterien', *Eranos Jahrbuch*, ed. O. Frobe-Kapteyn, II (1944) 397-98; M. Simon, 'The *Religionsgeschichtliche Schule*, Fifty Years Later', *Religious Studies* 2 (1975) 141; A.J.M. Wedderburn, 'Hellenistic Christian Traditions in Romans 6?' *NTS* 29 (1983) 344.
4 R. MacMullen, *Paganism in the Roman Empire* (New Haven and London: Yale University Press, 1981) 55. Cf. A.D. Nock, *Conversion* (Oxford: Clarendon, 1933) 70; Wagner, *Baptism* 253.
5 MacMullen, *Paganism* 55.
6 Wagner, *Baptism* 238-39; A.D. Nock, 'Eunuchs in Ancient Religion', *ARW* 23 (1925) 25-33.

the cymbal; I carried the sacred dish; I stole into the bridal chamber'.[1]

Firmicus gives an even more terse formula: 'I have eaten from the tambourine [*tympanos*], I have drunk from the cymbal, and I have mastered the secrets of Attis'.[2]

These formulae do not suggest a communal meal or one at which the god is eaten.[3] Nor is there any basis 'for supposing that the ritual conveyed special powers or immortality or union with the god'.[4] Klauck notes that 'a commemoration of Attis and his fate is not under consideration'.[5] However, the two formulae do not really support Klauck's conclusion, either.[6] Knowledge of what these acts meant must, finally, await further evidence.[7] It can be said, though, that they in no way appear connected with a god's death.

There is evidence for a kitchen attached to the Cybele temple at Piraeus,[8] but the significance of meals cooked in it is not clear. Shortly after noting this evidence, Kane sums up his examination of cult-meals thus:

> The few indications that we have found regarding the significance of such feasts have been couched in terms of social relaxation and pleasures and the giving of due honor to the gods. Nowhere in all this do we find any sacramental ritual which conveys special grace or powers.[9]

Conclusion

At the time of Paul, the central element in Attis' myth was his castration, not his death. Attestation of Attis' resurrection is

---

1   Clement of Alexandria, 'The Exhortation to the Greeks', *Clement of Alexandria* (trans. G.W. Butterworth; London: Heinemann; New York: Putnam, 1919) 2.14. Eleusinian influence is quite possible here. Cf. J.P. Kane, 'The Mithraic Cultic Meal' 34-42n142; Klauck, *Herrenmahl* 124.

2   Firmicus Maternus, *Firmicus Maternus: The Error of the Pagan Religions* (ACW, 37; trans. C.A. Forbes; New York and Ramsey, N.H.: Newman, 1970) 18.1.

3   Kane, 'The Mithraic Cultic Meal', 341-42n142; Klauck, *Herrenmahl* 124.

4   Kane, 'The Mithraic Cultic Meal', 341-42n142

5   Klauck, *Herrenmahl* 124.

6   Klauck, *Herrenmahl* 124.

7   J.G. Machen, *The Origin of Paul's Religion* (New York: Macmillan, 1921) 230; Metzger, 'Methodology' 15.

8   W.S. Ferguson, 'The Attic Orgeones', *HTR* 37 (1944) 114.

9   Kane, 'The Mithraic Cultic Meal', 329.

slender in the extreme. There is no evidence for regarding the
death as a participatory event. Influence on Paul, therefore,
seems unlikely.

Adonis

Baptism into Adonis

Nothing suggests that baptism was practiced by followers of
Adonis.

Adonis' Death

Adonis' death is clearly attested by the ancient sources.[1]

Adonis' Resurrection

The best evidence for Adonis' resurrection is contained in
Lucian. Lucian states that the worshippers at Byblos mourn
for Adonis, make offerings to him, and then pretend he is alive,
bringing him into the air.[2]

Apollodorus,[3] following Panysasis, reports that Aphrodite
had the infant Adonis in a chest and gave him to Persephone
to safeguard. But, taken by his beauty, Persephone refused to
return him. Finally, Zeus ordained that Adonis should spend a
third of the year with Aphrodite, a third with Persephone, and
have a third for himself. (Adonis chose, however to spend his
third with Aphrodite.) This tale would seem to imply some sort
of death-and-rebirth pattern, but as it is described in Apollodorus, it is more akin to change of residence.[4] This conclusion
is supported by the fact that Apollodorus ends his account of
Adonis with the latter's death by a boar.[5]

---

1 Ammianus Marcellinus 19.1.11; Apollodorus, *Bibliotheca* 3.14.4; Aristophanes,
   Lysistrata 388-98; Athenaeus, *Deipnosophistae* II 696; Lucian, *De Dea Syria* 6-9;
   Ovid, *Met.* 10.298-559, 708-39; Plutarch, *Alcibiades* 18.3, 7; *Nicias* 7; *Quaest. Conviv.* IV.5; Theocritus, *Idylls* 15.
2 Lucian, *De Dea Syria* 6. The precise meaning of the phrase continues to be
   unclear. Cf. N. Robertson, 'The Ritual of the Dying God in Cyprus and Syro-
   Palestine', *HTR* 75 (1982) 333n59, for recent discussion of the problem (but in
   Robertson's Burkert citation read n15 instead of n0). Nilsson, *Geschichte* 2.650n4,
   believes this represents Osirian influence.
3 Apollodorus, *Bibliotheca* 3.14.4.
4 Wagner, *Baptism* 181.
5 Apollodoros, *Bibliotheca* 3.14.4.

This ending shows that, in the author's eyes, Adonis' journey to join Persephone did not constitute a death. Indeed, the journey is first mentioned as a kind of protective measure for Adonis.[1]

Theocritus exhibits a similar attitude toward Adonis' passage between the lower and upper worlds. He never attributes resurrection or reanimation to Adonis. Instead the demigod's appearance is depicted as a simple return. Theocritus writes:

> Aphrodite with playthings of gold,
> Now out of eternal Acheron the soft-footed Hours
> Have led Adonis back to you in the twelfth month.[2]

Here Adonis' arrival is not a return to life, but simply a return. Later, his shuttling back and forth between the two worlds is remarked upon:

> O dear Adonis, both earth and Acheron do you frequent,
> Unique, as they tell us, among demigods.[3]

That the issue here is not life/death, but coming/going is shown finally by the end of the song offered in Adonis' honor:

> Bless us next year as well, dear Adonis. Joyful are we
> At your coming now, and joyful will be your return.[4]

Ovid tells a story about Adonis which omits any reference at all to a passage between worlds.[5] According to the *Metamorphoses*, Adonis is killed by a boar and remains dead. (In this, Ovid agrees with Apollodorus' ending.) As a monument to her grief, Aphrodite raises up the anemone from Adonis' blood, but he does not experience a resurrection.[6]

---

1 On the conflated nature of Apollodorus' account, cf. Wagner, *Baptism* 182.
2 Theocritus, *The Idylls of Theocritus* (trans. T. Sargent; New York and London: Norton, 1982) 60.
3 Theocritus, *The Idylls of Theocritus* 61.
4 Theocritus, *The Idylls of Theocritus* 62. On the absence of a resurrection motif in *Idyll* 15, see A.S.F. Gow, 'The *Adoniazusae* of Theocritus', *JHS* 58 (1938) 182.
5 Ovid, *Met.* 10.298-559, 708-39.
6 Cf. Wagner, *Baptism* 183.

As for the other ancient sources, they refer only to the death: Ammianus Marcellinus,[1] Aristophanes,[2] Athenaeus,[3] Plutarch,[4] and Sappho.[5] Even Firmicus Maternus describes Adonis' death without alluding to any resurrection.[6]

Dying and Rising with Adonis
No ancient text suggests participation by devotees in the fate of Adonis. Lucian, who comes closest, still mentions only the pretense that he is alive, and the celebration thereof.

Cultic Meals
There are no cultic meals connected with Adonis.[7]

Conclusion
There is little to form a basis from which Adonis worship could have exerted an influence on Paul. Evidence for a resurrection is slender and late,[8] and there are no indications of the kind of identification with the destiny of the lord which Paul describes in Romans 6. Neither did Adonis worship have the potential for influencing interpretations of the Eucharist.

Isis and Osiris

Baptism into Isis and Osiris
The washing ceremony of the Isis-initiate and the sprinkling rites practiced in the Osirian cult both function as simple acts of purification.[9]

---

1 Ammianus Marcellinus, 19.1.11.
2 Aristophanes, *Lysistrata* 388-98.
3 Athenaeus, *Deipnosophistae* 2.69b.
4 Plutarch, *Alcibiades* 18.2-3, *Nicias* 13.7, *Quaest. Conviv.* 4.5.
5 Sappho, *Fragments* 83.
6 Firmicus Maternus, *De errore* 9.1
7 Cf. Klauck, *Herrenmahl* 152-53; Wagner, *Baptism* 201-207.
8 Cf. Burkert, *Structure and History* 101; Nilsson, *Geschichte* 2.650n4.
9 For the washing ceremony of the Isis-initiate, cf. H.A.A. Kennedy, *St. Paul and the Mystery Religions* (London: Hodder and Stoughton, 1913) 229-30; R. Schnackenburg, *Baptism in the thought of St. Paul* (trans. G.R. Beasley-Murray; Oxford: Blackwell, 1964). On the sprinkling rites practiced in the Osirian cult, see Wagner, *Baptism* 127-35.

Death of Isis and Osiris
No attestation exists for Isis as a dying goddess.[1] That Osiris was regarded as a god who died is, however, clear (see next two sections below).

Resurrection of Isis and Osiris
Since Isis does not die, there is no need for her to be resurrected. With Osiris, though, the issue becomes complicated. Apuleius does not refer to any sort of resuscitation on Osiris' part. The best evidence is in Plutarch's description of the following Egyptian rite: priests and those in charge of the robes go to the seacoast at night; there they open a sacred chest, pour in some water, and proclaim Osiris risen; then they mix the water with soil, spices, and incense, mold a crescent, and adorn it.[2]

However, in recounting the myth of Isis and Osiris[3] (as opposed to the above ritual), Plutarch's evidence is a bit more ambiguous. He says only that at some point after the reassembly of his body, Osiris came to his son Horus from Hades.[4] This vagueness accords with what we know of earlier Egyptian views of Osiris' status after his death. Frankfort summarizes the god's role in Pharaonic Eqypt by saying that he

> was not a 'dying god' but—if the paradox be permitted—a dead god. There is no evidence that his death was represented in ritual; at every ceremony Osiris appeared as a god who had passed through death, who survived in the sense that he was not utterly destroyed, but who did not return to life. His resurrection meant his entry upon life in the Beyond . . .[5]

Dying and Rising with Isis and Osiris
Since Isis does not die or rise, there is no hint of her worshippers dying and rising with her. When Apuleius has Lucius

---

1 Cf. T. Wilson, *St. Paul and Paganism* (Edinburgh: Clark, 1927) 95.
2 Plutarch, *De Iside et Osiride* 39=366F.
3 Plutarch, *De Iside et Osiride* 12-19=355D-358E.
4 Plutarch, *De Iside et Osiride* 19=358B.
5 H. Frankfort, *Kingship and the Gods* (Chicago: The University of Chicago Press, 1948) 185. Cf. also Burkert, *Structure and History* 101; H. Frankfort, *Ancient Egyptian Religion* (New York: Columbia University Press, 1948) 102-103; Metzger, 'Methodology', 20-21; A. Oepke, 'ἐγείρω', *TDNT* 2.335; Wagner, *Baptism* 119-20.

say 'I approached near unto hell',[1] nothing suggests that this
has happened through sharing Isis' (or Osiris') experience.
The statement 'it was in her [Isis'] power both to damn and to
save all persons'[2] shows Isis in control of the powers of life and
death, but Apuleius does not indicate that such control involves
her dying-and-rising.[3] It is true that, in the same sentence,
Lucius is told that entering Isis' service is 'like to a voluntary
death and a difficult recovery to health'. Shortly after, we read
that 'if anywhere there were any at the point of death and at
the end and limit of their life, so that they were capable to
receive the dread secrets of the goddess, it was in her power by
divine providence to make them as it were new-born and to
reduce them to the path of health'. Despite the suggestiveness
of all this, dying-and-rising with Isis never becomes an issue,
and the admonition to Lucius remains at the level of mere
metaphor.

It has been argued that when Lucius appears 'like unto the
sun'[4] after his first initiation, he has become Osiris. This, in
turn, could imply that he has died and risen with Osiris. However, such an interpretation must remain speculative.[5]

---

1 Apuleius, *The Golden Ass* (LCL; trans. W. Adlington; revised by S. Gaselee
   London: William Heinemann; New York: Putnam, 1919) XI.23.

2 Apuleius, *The Golden Ass* XI.21.

3 The reference to voluntary death and subsequent recovery (*The Golden Ass* XI.21)
   remains intriguing. There is no connection at this point with the death and/or re-
   birth of a deity, but nonetheless, this passage helps to place the Isis-Osiris cult in a
   relation to Pauline Chrisitanity that Ludwig Wittgenstein might call a 'family-
   resemblance'.

4 Apuleius, *The Golden Ass* XI.24.

5 H. Gressmann, *Die orientalischen Religionen im hellenistisch-romischen
   Zeitalter* (Berlin and Leipzig: Walter de Gruyter & Co., 1930) 42n1, and Wengst,
   Christologische Formeln 40, claim that Lucius' passage through all the elements
   (*The Golden Ass* XI.23) follows the passage of the sun, i.e. Osiris. But Wagner
   points out that the identification of Osiris with the sun was late and tenuous, *Baptism* 105n91. Wengst maintains that this is not a difficulty, since Osiris is inter-
   changeable with Sarapis, and the latter was definitely identified with the sun,
   Christologische Formeln 40. But Apuleius does not seem to have regarded these two
   gods as equivalent (he mentions Sarapis only at *The Golden Ass* XI.9). Moreover,
   that the two names could sometimes be exchanged did not obscure a fairly definite
   functional distinction; cf. J.E. Stambaugh, *Sarapis under the early Ptolemies*
   (EPRO, 25; Leiden: Brill, 1972) 44-52, esp. 46. Sarapis remained a god who did not
   die and rise, Wagner, *Baptism* 105n91. Added to these considerations is the fact
   that Lucius' first initiation is directed toward Isis, not Osiris. The hymn of praise
   to Isis in *The Golden Ass* XI.25 shows that resort to Osiris is unnecessary here, for
   the Goddess herself illuminates the sun, treads Tartarus underfoot, and has the

The first of Lucius' two Osiris-initiations is described simply by saying that he 'was initiate into the ceremonies of the great god, which were done in the night'.[1] The second initiation is not described at all. We therefore have no real ground on which to conclude that some dying-and-rising took place during these initiations.

Neither does Plutarch's *De Iside et Osiride* contain any material on dying-and-rising with a god. The recounting of the myth focuses on the gods themselves (rather than on initiates), and besides, never actually addresses Osiris' resuscitation. Plutarch says only that at some point after his reassembly, Osiris came to Horus from Hades. As for rituals in which the believers pariticipate in the god's destiny, the procedure described above, involving the shaping of a crescent, comes closest. But this can hardly be said to constitute dying-and-rising with Osiris.

Firmicus Maternus portrays the Osirians lamenting the god's statue on a bier, whereupon a light is brought in and a priest whispers:

> Rejoice, O mystai! Lo, our god appears as saved!
> And we shall find salvation, springing from our woes.[2]

Here Osiris' salvation is a prototype for the worshippers', but the god's death is not said to be vicarious, nor does the text set forth a pattern of dying and rising with him.[3] In light of Osiris' lordship of the dead (see below), this should probably be interpreted as a promise of well-being in the next world (note the future tense).[4]

Firmicus' text also contains, a bit later, the words 'So you should die as he [Osiris] dies, and you should live as he lives'![5] This is, of course, highly provocative, but the context indicates that here Firmicus is speaking ironically. The two sentences immediately prior to the one just quoted read as follows:

elements as her slaves. The match with Lucius' initiatory journey is quite satisfactory and renders needless eisegetical references to other deities.

1 Apuleius, *The Golden Ass* XI.28.
2 Firmicus Maternus, *De errore* 22.1.
3 For a list of those who believe 22.1 does establish pattern of dying and rising with the god, cf. Wagner, *Baptism* 96-97nn48-51.
4 Wedderburn, 'Hellenistic Christian Traditions' 345.
5 Firmicus Maternus, *De errore* 22.3

> You rescue your god, you put together the stony limbs that lie
> there, you set in position an insensible stone. Your god
> should thank you, should repay you with equivalent gifts,
> should be willing to make you his partner.[1]

Firmicus' point is that the Osirians do *not*, in fact, share partnership with their god, and do not die or live with him. This
interpretation makes more sense, given the context of angry
accusations, than an interpretation imputing to Firmicus the
belief that Osirians relate to Osiris in the same way that
Christians relate to Christ.[2]

Older evidence for dying-and-rising with Osiris is scanty at
best. As lord of the dead, Osiris could be looked to as a prototype
and protector of, first Pharaoh, and later all men. It is clear,
however, that the life which one shares with Osiris remains in
the hereafter. From the Pyramid Texts we read:

> Oh, King Teti, how lovely is this, how great is this
> Which thy father Osiris has done for thee.
> He has ceded his throne to thee
> So that thou commandest those with hidden seats ...
> And guidest the Venerable Ones ... [3]

The Venerable Ones with hidden seats are the dead,[4] and the
dead Pharoah comes to share Osiris' rule over them.

Even after the democratization of Osiris' role (according to
which any man, not just the Pharaoh, could hope to be identified with Osiris after death),[5] the separation of his minions
from the land of the living is clear:

> They are all thine, all those who come to thee,
> Great and small, they belong to thee;
> Those who live upon earth, they all reach thee,
> Thou art their master, ... [6]

None of these Isiac or Osirian texts leads to an interpretation
of dying and rising with the deity. Isis does not die and rise. As
for Osiris, he dies but does not really rise; rather, he becomes

---

1 Firmicus Maternus, *De errore* 22.3
2 Wagner, *Baptism* 97.
3 Frankfort, *Kingship and the Gods* 111.
4 Frankfort, *Kingship and the Gods* 111.
5 Cf. Frankfort, *Ancient Egyptian Religion* 103-105; Wagner *Baptism* 123.
6 Frankfort, *Ancient Egyptian Religion* 103-104.

lord of the dead and is joined by his devotees after their own deaths.

Cult Meal

There is some evidence for meals in Isis-worship,[1] but there is none to connect them with a deity's death, or to suggest that they established the kind of special bond with the deity about which Paul talks.[2]

There are three instances in which Apuleius refers to meals which could be cultic. The first occurs following Lucius' initiation under Isis. After he is presented to the group, a celebration is held to celebrate the start of his life of devotion: 'Then they began to solemnise the feast, the nativity of my holy order, with sumptuous banquets and pleasant meats ...'[3] Then, on the third day, the celebration continues: 'the third day was likewise celebrated with like ceremonies, with a religious dinner, and with all the consummation of the adept order'.[4] The phrase 'nativity of my holy order' has been interpreted to mean a re-birth from the death which Lucius has just experienced.[5] However, the 'new man' motif seems limited here to Lucius' status as a devotee of the goddess. The 'birthday' being celebrated signals the start of his new role in life.[6] If Apuleius had wanted to attach this directly to Lucius' approach to Hades and thus to a more broadly conceived rebirth, he could have done so.

The phrase 'religious dinner' seems to mean simply a dinner in honor of a deity, of which we have many examples.[7]

---

1 Klauck, *Herrenmahl* 127-28; cf. also Apuleius, *The Isis-Book* (EPRO, 39; ed. J.G. Griffiths; Leiden: Brill, 1975) 318; L. Vidman, *Isis und Sarapis bei den Griechen und Römern* (Berlin: de Gruyter, 1970) 87-88.

2 M. Dibelius, 'The Isis Initiation in Apuleius and Related Initiatory Rites', *Conflict at Colossae* (Sources for Biblical Study 4; rev. edn; ed. and trans. F.O. Francis and W.A. Meeks; Missoula, MT: SBL and Scholars Press, 1975) 81.

3 Apuleius, *The Golden Ass* XI.24.

4 Apuleius, *The Golden Ass* XI.24.

5 Apuleius, *The Golden Ass* XI.23; cf. also *idem*, *Isis-Book* 317; W. L. Knox, *Some Hellenistic Elements in Primitive Christianity* (London: Milford [British Academy], 1944) 91.

6 Wagner, *Baptism* 113; cf. Klauck, *Herrenmahl* 131.

7 Apuleius, *Isis-Book* 318-19; cf. Klauck, *Herrenmahl* ch. 7.

The same applies to the third instance of a possibly cultic meal.[1]

There is thus no basis for attributing theophagy to the worship of Isis–Osiris.[2] Neither does it become evident that meals bind the believer to the deity in the sort of special, exclusive manner of which Paul speaks in 1 Cor. 10.20-22.

Conclusion

From the above overview of the worship of Isis and Osiris, it appears unlikely that their cult could have had a significant influence on Paul.

Eleusis

Baptism into Demeter and Persephone

There is no indication that the bathing undertaken by Eleusinian initiates was more than a preliminary purification. It preceded the actual rites by several days, and no ancient source attaches special significance to it.[3]

Death and Resurrection of Demeter and Persephone

While Demeter and Persephone do descend to Hades, they are never portrayed as undergoing an actual death experience with which initiates might identify. Their activity, like Adonis', is more a journey than a dying and rising.[4]

Dying and Rising with Demeter and Persephone

Pindar and Sophocles speak of the devotee visiting Hades.[5] However, it is not clear that there was an imitation of Demeter's quest.[6] 'A comparison of the fate of the mystes with the

---

1 Prior to his second initiation (this time under Osiris), Lucius has a dream in which a priest tells him of a religious banquet, *The Golden Ass* XI.27.

2 Klauck, *Herrenmahl* 131, esp. n277.

3 Wagner, *Baptism* 71-73. Cf. also Burkert, *Greek Religion* 287; Kennedy, *St. Paul* 229-30.

4 Cf. Klauck, *Herrenmahl* 105.

5 Burkert, *Greek Religion* 289.

6 Wagner, *Baptism* 75-79. The one instance in which such imitation does seem to be dictated is a preliminary purification rite, where the initiate sits, like Demeter, with head veiled and on a stool covered by a ram's fleece, Burkert, *Greek Religion* 286.

fate of Kore [Demeter] is nowhere articulated'.[1]

The nature of the ritual itself contributes to skepticism regarding such imitation. First there is the fact that the initiates were not allowed to see the ritual; only those in attendance for at least the second time could do so, and these were called watchers.[2] This name suggests that the devotee's role as witness, not as imitator, was paramount. Second is the lack of a suitable opening in the earth for enacting a drama of descent.[3] Third, what we know about the course of the ritual suggests a reference to Demeter dipping a child into the hearth,[4] an act which is not copied and which is not precisely a part of the quest for Persephone. Fourth, none of the climactic events of the ritual involve imitation by the devotees.[5]

Cultic Meal
Although meals did play a significant role in the Eleusinian mysteries,[6] they were not connected to the death of a deity (either as a memorial or as theophagy).[7]

Conclusion
Because Demeter and Persephone did not die, and because there is no evidence for an imitation of their actions, it seems improbable that the Eleusinian cult would have influenced Paul's interpretation of Jesus' death.

General Conclusion

It has been shown that each of the mystery cults examined above was unlikely to have exerted much influence on Paul. At this point it is appropriate to add several general considerations distinguishing the Mysteries and the Pauline interpretation of Jesus' death. The Mystery deities' deaths are not

---

1 Wagner, *Baptism* 81. Cf. also Wedderburn, 'Hellenistic Christian Traditions' 344.
2 Burkert, *Greek Religion* 287.
3 Burkert, *Greek Religion* 288.
4 Burkert, *Greek Religion* 288.
5 The hierophant calls upon Kore, announces the birth of Brimos, and cuts an ear of corn. Cf. Burkert, *Greek Religion* 288.
6 Klauck, *Herrenmahl* 94-106.
7 Klauck, *Herrenmahl* 105.

vicarious.[1] According to the Mysteries, the deities die unwillingly rather than obediently.[2] The gods are not historical personages, as was Jesus.[3] The Mysteries contain few social or ethical elements.[4] Finally, they possess no apocalyptic framework.[5]

1 Wagner, *Baptism* 117.

2 Nash, *Christianity* 172.

3 Althaus, *Römer* 57; Metzger, 'Methodology' 13.

4 Davies, *Paul and Rabbinic Judaism* 90; Wiens, 'Mystery Concepts' 1279.

5 E.R. Bevan, 'Mystery Religions', *The History of Christianity in the Light of Modern Knowledge* (New York: Harcourt, Brace, 1929) 113; Wengst, *Christologische Formeln* 40.

   Unfortunately, A.J.M. Wedderburn's article 'The Soteriology of the Mysteries and Pauline Baptismal Theology', *NovT* 29 (1987) 53-72, came into my hands too late to be incorporated into this chapter. It is gratifying to note, however, that Wedderburn's skepticism regarding connections between Paul and the Mysteries accords with the findings presented here.

Chapter 5

PAUL'S DOCTRINE OF SALVATION
AND THE CONCEPT OF THE NOBLE DEATH

Introduction

This chapter can be divided into four sections. The first
outlines the thesis that Paul's interpretation of Jesus' death is
indebted to martyrology. It does so by discussing several of the
authors who have taken this position. The second deals with *2
Maccabees* (probably 1st century BCE), the older of the two
most important texts for this thesis (the younger is *4 Maccabees*, 20-54 CE). This section finds that, in *2 Maccabees,* one
martyr's death as vicarious, but not in an expiatory fashion;
rather, it is vicarious in a mimetic or imitative fashion. (By
'vicarious' I mean that which is on behalf of others, and by
'expiatory' I mean that which cancels the effects of sin.) Three
more elements besides vicariousness are isolated as significant
aspects of martyrdom in *2 Maccabees.* They are: obedience, a
military context, and overcoming physical vulnerability. This
cluster of four elements is termed the Noble Death. In the
third section, the Noble Death is traced through *4 Maccabees*.
There, a fifth element is also located, although it is ancillary.
This is the application of sacrificial metaphors to the act of
martyrdom. The fourth section examines the Noble Death as
it appears in Paul.

The Martyr Thesis

In *Märtyrer und Gottesknecht*,[1] E. Lohse argues the importance of Palestinian, Jewish martyrology for early Christian[2] and (to some extent) specifically Pauline[3] interpretations of Jesus' vicarious, expiatory death. At the outset, Lohse excludes Hellenism and Hellenistic Judaism from consideration. The first is eliminated because it views death as a natural event rather than as a consequence of sin,[4] and the second because it essentially inherits that attitude (as shown by Philo and Josephus).[5] Nevertheless, it is in two Hellenistic Jewish texts, *2* and *4 Maccabees*, that Lohse finds the earliest examples of vicarious deaths on the part of martyrs. He maintains that the Hellenistic influence on these texts is not critical, since their true indebtedness is to Palestinian Judaism.[6] Lohse calls on Midrashic and Targumic writings to support his claim,[7] but has to admit that the only evidence he can find stems from the later, Amoraic period.[8] Continuing his effort to prove that the martyrology of *2* and *4 Maccabees* reflects pre-Christian, Palestinian, Jewish thought, Lohse then tries to reconstruct a Jewish tradition which he believes surrounded the death of the righteous.[9] At last, however, he must return to the Maccabean texts themselves in order to anchor this presumed tradition in pre-Christian times.[10] This movement gives his argument a certain circularity. Lohse does attempt to enlist *Testament of Benjamin* 3.8 as corroborating, pre-Christian

---

1 J.S. Pobee, *Persecution and Martyrdom in the Theology of Paul* (JSNTS, 6: Sheffield, England: JSOT Press, 1985) 49, reiterates but does not develop Lohse's thesis. His approach can be discerned from the following: 'The idea of vicarious suffering and propitiation was not unfamiliar to pre-Christian Judaism, as 2 Macc. 7.18, 32, 38 and 4 Macc. 6.28-29 amply demonstrate'. It is precisely the 'ampleness' of this demonstration which is being called into question here.

2 Lohse, *Märtyrer passim*, especially 66-78.

3 Lohse, *Märtyrer* 147-62.

4 Lohse, *Märtyrer* 9-10.

5 Lohse, *Märtyrer* 11-12.

6 Lohse, *Märtyrer* 68-69, 71.

7 Lohse, *Märtyrer* 72-78.

8 Lohse, *Märtyrer* 77. Cf. the critique by Wengst, *Christologische Formeln* 64n44. Cf. also Gubler, *Die Deutungen* 250.

9 Lohse, *Märtyrer* 78-87.

10 Lohse, *Märtyrer* 85.

evidence,[1] but problems with Christian influence[2] and textual transmission[3] figure against this.

Lohse thus fails to demonstrate his thesis regarding the pre-Christian, Palestinian, Jewish origins of 2 and 4 Maccabees. This failure leaves him in the ironic position of insisting that a non-Hellenistic form of Judaism is the source of Jewish thinking on vicarious, expiatory death, while actually finding that two Hellenistic, Jewish texts (2 and 4 Maccabees) contain the earliest intertestamental examples of such deaths. The irony of Lohse's position is compounded by the fact that, in his view, only 4 Maccabees really contains examples of vicarious, expiatory death, and that text is even more Hellenistic than 2 Maccabees.[4]

---

1 Lohse, *Märtyrer* 85-87.

2 Gubler, *Die Deutungen* 251; M. de Jonge, 'Christian influence in the Testaments of the Twelve Patriarchs', *Studies on the Testaments of the Twelve Patriarchs* (ed. M. de Jonge; SVTP 3; Leiden: E.J. Brill, 1975) 193-246; H.C. Kee, 'Testaments of the Twelve Patriarchs', *The Old Testament Pseudepigrapha* (ed. J.H. Charlesworth; 2 vols.; Garden City, New York: Doubleday, 1983) 1.826n3b; Lohse, *Märtyrer* 86; Popkes, *Christus Traditus* 47-55; Wengst, *Christologische Formeln* 65n50. Cf. also Rese, 'Überprüfung' 24-27. For a history of the debate on Christian influence in the Testament of the Twelve Patriarchs, see H.D. Slingerland, *The Testaments of the Twelve Patriarchs: A Critical History of Research* (SBLDS, 21; Missoula, Mont.: Scholars Press, 1975).

3 J.J. Collins, 'Testaments', *Jewish Writings of the Second Temple Period* (Compendia Rerum Iudaicarum ad Novum Testamentum; section two; vol. 2; ed. M. Stone; Assen: Van Gorcum; Philadelphia: Fortress, 1984) 331-33; O. Eissfeldt, *The Old Testament* (trans. P.R. Ackroyd; New York and Evanston, Ill.: Harper & Row, 1965) 636; H.J. de Jonge, 'Die Textüberlieferung der Testamente der zwölfe Patriarchen', *Studies on the Testaments of the Twelve Patriarchs* 45-62; Kee, 'Testaments of the Twelve Patriarchs' 775-76. Cf. Also H. de Jonge, 'The earliest traceable stage of the textual tradition of the Testaments of the Twelve Patriarchs', *Studies on the Testaments of the Twelve Patriarchs* 63-86; M. de Jonge, *Testamenta XII Patriarchum* (Pseudepigrapha Veteris Testamenti Graece 1; Leiden: E.J. Brill, 1964) VII-XVI; *idem, The Testaments of the Twelve Patriarchs* (Van Gorcums theologische Bibliothek 25; 2nd edn; Assen and Amsterdam: Van Gorcum, 1975) 13-36; T. Kortweg, 'Further observation of the transmission of the text', *Studies on the Testaments of the Twelve Patriarchs* 161-73.

4 Lohse, *Märtyrer* 68, believes that the thought of expiatory death 'is not explicitly stated in Second Maccabees, but nevertheless the thought of representation is clearly expressed (7, 37-38)'.

    The following authors attest to the sophisticated nature of the Greek in which *4 Maccabees* was written: U. Breitenstein, *Beobachtungen zu Sprache, Stil und Gedankengut des Vierten Makkabäerbuchs* (2nd edn; Basel: Schwabe, 1978) chs. 1–3; M. Hadas, commentary in *The Third and Fourth Books of Maccabees* (New York: Published for the Dropsie College for Hebrew and Cognate Learning by

K. Wengst offers a solution to Lohse's dilemma by simply abandoning the latter's thesis about Palestinian Judaism.[1] The evidence points to Hellenistic Judaism as the source, and Wengst believes the evidence should be followed.[2] At this point he comes close to another work written at almost the same time by S.K. Williams. Williams, too, focuses on the books of the Maccabees and he, too, concludes that they are indebted to Hellenistic Judaism for their interpretations of martyrdom.[3] Both authors ultimately turn to Hellenism itself for clarification, but both leave problems in the wake of their analyses. Wengst treats the whole issue in less than a page, pointing out that Thucydides, Plato, Epictetus, and Philostratus all contain examples of vicarious deaths.[4] This leaves questions about the transmission, form, and function of the concept. Williams makes a closer examination, but lands finally on Euripides as the nearest parallel to *4 Maccabees*.[5] Again, this leaves a host of questions as to how such interpretations of death might have traveled over the centuries, and just what the component

Harper and Row, 1953) 100-3; E. Norden, *Die Antike Kunstprosa* (5th edn; vol. 1; Darmstadt: Wissenschaftliche Buchgesellschaft, 1958) 418-20; C.C. Torrey, *The Apocryphal Literature* (New Haven: Yale University Press, 1945) 105; R.B. Townshend, '4 Maccabees', *The Apocrypha and Pseudepigrapha of the Old Testament* (ed. R.H. Charles; 2 vols; Oxford: Clarendon, 1913) 2.655; Williams, *Jesus' Death* 186.

     Hadas, *Maccabees* 115-18, thinks *4 Maccabees* was influenced by classical Greek philosophy. The following authors think it was influenced by Hellenistic philosophy: G.W.E. Nickelsburg, *Jewish Literature between the Bible and Mishnah* (Philadelphia: Fortress Press, 1981) 223-24; V.C. Pfitzner, *Paul and the Agon Motif* (SNT, 16; Leiden: Brill, 1967) 57-69; R. Renehan, 'The Greek Philosophic Background of Fourth Maccabees', *Rheinisches Museum für Philologie* 115 (1972) 222-38; Townshend, '4 Maccabees' 2.657, 662-63; Williams, *Jesus' Death* 187.

     On the interpenetration of Hellenism and Judaism generally cf. M. Hengel, *Judaism and Hellenism* (2 vols; trans. J. Bowman; Philadelphia: Fortress, 1973).

1 Wengst, *Christologische Formeln* 57.
2 Lohse's sharp distinction between Palestinian and Hellenistic Judaism constitutes an outmoded approach in any case. Cf. *inter alia* Hengel, *Judaism and Hellenism*; M. Smith, *Palestinian Parties and Politics that Shaped the Old Testament World* (Lectures on the history of religions, new series, 9; New York: Columbia University Press, 1971) ch. 3.
3 Williams, *Jesus' Death* 165-202.
4 Wengst, *Christologische Formeln* 67.
5 Williams, *Jesus' Death* 153-61. It should be noted here that, despite my criticism of Williams, his book was instrumental in provoking this entire investigation.

parts might have been. Finally, it should be noted that both Wengst and Williams are concerned with pre-Pauline, primitive Christianity, while the focus here is on Paul.

Nevertheless, in light of the provocative findings of all three authors named above, a careful look at 2 and 4 *Maccabees* is in order.

2 Maccabees

Wengst asserts that 2 *Maccabees* contains the concept of vicarious, expiatory death. 2 *Macc.* 7.32, he says, refers not only to 'the sins of the martyrs themselves ... but those of the entire people'.[1] This shows that the martyr was thought to be particularly capable of calling upon God for mercy towards the people (7.37). Furthermore, the prayer in 7.38 'that through the martyrdom of the brothers the wrath of God over the people may come to an end', makes plain 'that here the thought of representative, expiatory death is present'.[2]

Wengst's argument is flawed on several counts, however. First, 2 *Macc.* 7.32 gives no indication that the martyrs are suffering because of others' sins. In fact, it says the opposite. In the words of the youngest brother: '... we are suffering because of our own sins'. It is true that the author is probably not suggesting the martyrs themselves have sinned.[3] Nonetheless there is no hint of a special representative function being played by the martyrs here. Rather, 7.32 seems to point to a form of 'group solidarity'.[4] It is portraying not the martyrs' special status as representatives of the people, but the extent to which they are at one with the people.

As for the martyrs' peculiar ability to invoke God's mercy, this thesis is called into question by 2 *Macc.* 8.2-4. There Judas Maccabeus and his guerillas call on God in terms very similar

---

1 Wenst, *Christologische Formeln* 69. H.-W. Surkau, *Märtyrien in Jüdischer und frühchristlicher Zeit* (FRLANT, 54; Göttingen: Vandenhoeck & Ruprecht, 1938) 59, argues that 2 *Macc.* 7.6 also exhibits the doctrine of vicarious, expiatory death. For a detailed rebuttal of Surkau's argument, cf. Williams, *Jesus' Death* 82-85. Cf. also J.A. Goldstein, *II Maccabees* (AB, 41a; Garden City, New York: Doubleday & Co., 1983) 296, 317.

2 Wengst, *Christologische Formeln* 69.

3 Williams, *Jesus' Death* 79n29.

4 Williams, *Jesus' Death* 79n29.

to those of 7.37. Just as the youngest brother asks God 'to show mercy soon to our nation', so Judas asks him 'to have mercy on the city'. If, indeed, martyrs can call on God's mercy in *2 Maccabees*, then it seems equally true that those in no immediate danger can do likewise. Finally, one must also doubt Wengst's opinion that the Greek word *en* in 7.38 is instrumental (cf. the 'through' in Wengst's paraphrase quoted above). More likely is a locative sense which asks God simply to stop his wrath at the point of the brothers' deaths.[1] Such an interpretation is supported by 7.37 and 8.2-4. The former, as seen, is a straightforward plea that mercy come soon. The latter also makes this request; moreover, its line of argument sheds further light on the interpretation of 7.38.

> They besought the Lord to look upon the people who were oppressed by all, and to have pity on the temple which had been profaned by ungodly men, and to have mercy on the city which was being destroyed and about to be leveled to the ground, and to hearken to the blood that cried out to him and to remember also the lawless destruction of the innocent babies and the blasphemies committed against his name and to show his hatred of evil. (*2 Macc.* 8.2-4)

Martyrological phenomena like blood which cries out (8.3) and the murder of babies are listed alongside non-martyrological events like oppression, profanation, destruction of property, and blasphemy.[2] This makes it all the less likely that an expiatory effect is attached to the shedding of innocent blood in *2 Macc.* 7. Rather, the totality of evils wrought by Antiochus—of whatever kind—is being held up to God as evidence that his people have suffered enough. When the last brother makes his prayer in 7.38, he, like Judas, is saying: let the anger stop here.[3]

The brothers' deaths are not, therefore, vicarious, expiatory ones. The brothers do not regard their deaths as special, but as

---

1 Williams, *Jesus' Death* 85-90.

2 Williams, *Jesus' Death* 88.

3 Goldstein, *II Maccabees* 315-16; S. Zeitlin, commentary in *The Second Book of Maccabees* (ed. S. Zeitlin; trans. S. Tedesche; New York: Published for the Dropsie College for Hebrew and Cognate Learning by Harper & Brothers, 1954) 159.

   It is revealing that *after* the prayer at *2 Macc.* 7.37-38, Judas must still ask for essentially the same thing (8.2-4).

of a piece with the sufferings of the whole people. They do not proclaim their innocence, but rather their guilt (whether conceived personally or collectively). They ask only that with their deaths, the suffering end. No one will benefit because of their deaths *per se*, but simply because God will have ceased his wrath with the latter. He will consider that the overall punishment and discipline have reached a point of sufficiency. The martyrs' deaths, in this sense, simply happened to be at the end of a series of sufferings.

There is, however, one death in *2 Maccabees* which does appear to benefit others because of its own, inherent character. This is Eleazar's death. In a manner strongly reminiscent of Socrates,[1] Eleazar says at 6.28 that he will leave

> to the young a noble example of how to die a good death willingly and nobly for the revered and holy laws.

After Eleazar dies under torture, the author comments:

> so in this way he died, leaving in his death an example of nobility and a memorial of courage, not only to the young but to the great body of his nation (6.31).

Unlike the brothers' deaths, Eleazar's death is vicarious. It benefits others through providing them with a model. This fact in itself would constitute an important distinction between the brothers' deaths and that of Eleazar, even if one were to insist on interpreting the former as vicarious. For nothing in particular is singled out about the brothers' deaths which makes them special in their own terms; Eleazar's death, however, is special because it is a model or a paradigm. Eleazar offers a pattern of righteousness by remaining obedient despite Antiochus' tortures. In their own efforts to stay faithful to the 'holy laws', people need only to look to his example. His death is described almost as a precious bequest to the Jewish nation. By copying his behaviour, others draw benefit from it. The mode of vicariousness which his death possesses may therefore be called mimetic, since it is conveyed via the process of imitation.

2 Macc. 6.31 makes plain that the beneficiaries of Eleazar's vicarious death include all of his contemporary fellow-citizens. But *2 Macc.* 6.12-17 suggests that the martyrs' stories are

---

1 Goldstein, *II Maccabees* 285; Hadas, *Maccabees* 117.

being recounted so that the reading audience, too, may draw benefit from them. In 6.12 the audience is urged 'not to be depressed' by the calamitous events that ovetook the pious in chs. 5–6. God disciplines his people as they sin, clearing the slate step by step. But the Gentiles he allows to go on until they reach the 'full measure of their sins' (6.14), whereupon he presumably will destroy them.

Immediately after this exhortation, the author presents the story of the martyrs. This sequence implies that the story is being offered for the encouragement and strengthening of the reading audience. It will benefit the latter by showing it the proper way to bear torture and persecution (i.e. God's discipline). Indeed, 6.19-20 constitutes not merely an offer of encouragement but a hortatory claim on any who want to remain righteous:

> But he, welcoming death with honor rather than life with pollution, went up to the rack of his own accord, spitting out the flesh, as men ought to go who have the courage to refuse things that it is not right to taste, even for the natural love of life.

The audience cannot escape the purview of this call to death with honor, a call which is given power and credibility by the fact that Eleazar has set the example and shown beyond doubt that it can be followed. Through this example, he enables others to respond likewise.

The process whereby the audience models itself on the martyrs' story constitutes a different sort of re-enactment than that outlined by 6.28 and 6.31. There the emphasis is on the literal imitation of Eleazar's death by his contemporaries facing the Antiochene persecution. But with respect to the reading audience, the emphasis is on the imaginative re-enactment of all the deaths through following the story. (In this particular regard, a vicarious side to the brothers' deaths and that of their mother can be conceded.) The audience gains courage by mentally re-actualizing these martyrdoms, and thereby coming to understand that it could re-actualize them literally as well (especially since the protagonists are an old man, young boys, and a mother). Indeed, such imaginative re-enactment must be admitted as implicit even in literarily oriented exhortations like 6.28 and 6.31. There, too, an example must be worked through mentally before it can be appropriated as an example. One must have the full pattern clearly in mind before following it in terms of behaviour. In other words, it is necessary to have ingested the story imaginatively prior to leading one's life in accordance with it. This process will become clearer and more explicit in *4 Maccabees*.

Three more aspects of Eleazar's death may be singled out for special notice. First is obedience. This is what makes Eleazar's death admirable and a pattern. Although he could easily save himself with a simple pretense (6.21-23), he refuses, insisting on strict adherence to the Law and thus ensuring his death. Second is a military context. Eleazar is a casualty in Antiochus' war against (the majority of) the Judaeans. Antiochus has come at the head of an army. The martyrs are among the victims of his campaign. Third is the overcoming of physical vulnerability. The latter, obviously, is what Antiochus plays on in attempting to force Eleazar to comply, but the old man overcomes this vulnerability via his inner resources. Eleazar himself puts it most succinctly when he says at 6.30:

> I am enduring terrible sufferings in my body under this beating, but in my soul I am glad to suffer these things because I fear [God].

Conclusion

It has been found, then, that the brothers' deaths are not vicarious with regard to their contemporaries. Eleazar's death is mimetically vicarious with regard to his contemporaries. All of the deaths have a mimetically vicarious nature with regard to the reading audience. Four aspects of Eleazar's death—vicariousness, obedience, a military context, and overcoming physical vulnerability—have been isolated as possessing particular importance. The cluster of these four aspects may be termed the Noble Death. (A fifth, less important aspect, namely sacrifice, will be discussed below.) The Noble Death will be traced through *4 Maccabees* and Paul in the remaining two sections of this chapter.

4 Maccabees

This section will show that *4 Maccabees'* description of the martyrs' deaths contains the four aspects just isolated, plus a fifth: sacrificial metaphors. These aspects will be discussed sequentially and under separate headings.

Vicariousness

The martyrs' deaths are of benefit to others. One way in which this benefit is expressed is through sacrificial metaphors (dealt with below). However, these metaphors will be seen to be consciously figurative and secondary. The more fundamental, historically conceivable (if not historically accurate) mode of expressing vicariousness is once again the mimetic process.

Eleazer says that it would be 'irrational' if he were to abandon the law and become 'a pattern of impiety to the young' (6.18-19). He voices his determination to die obediently (6.20-21) and concludes with this call: 'Therefore, O children of Abraham, die nobly for your religion! The 'therefore' (*pros tauta*) which begins Eleazar's statement shows that he is not just calling on the people to die nobly, but to follow his 'pattern' (*typos*) and die nobly. The old man's invitation to others to re-enact his obedient death in their own lives is echoed by the author himself when, at 7.8, he says:

> Such should be those who are administrators of the law, shielding it with their own blood and sweat in sufferings even unto death.

At 9.6, the brothers refer to the old man as 'our aged instructor', and portray him as their model for pious suffering. Subsequently, the brothers serve as models for one another (9.23; 10.3; 10.16; 11.15; 12.16; 13.8-18).

In a wider sense, however, all the martyrs' deaths benefit the entire nation. Their example of obedience inspires a general adherence to the Law and thus defeats Antiochus: 'by reviving observance of the law in the homeland they ravaged the enemy' (18.4). This rather surprising connection of Torah-obedience and victory over the enemy is explained in 18.5.

> Since in no way whatever was he [Antiochus] able to compel the Israelites to become pagans and to abandon their ancestral customs, he left Jerusalem and marched against the Persians.

The Israelites, emulating the martyrs, refuse to give in to the tyrant's efforts to make them abandon the Torah. The sequence indicated by 18.4-5 (martyrs' deaths → general Torah-obedience → defeat of Antiochus) explains the otherwise puzzling statement at 1.11 that

> all people, even their torturers, marveled at their [the martyrs'] courage and endurance, and they became the cause of the downfall of tyranny over their nation. By their endurance they conquered the tyrant ...

The martyrs become the 'cause of the downfall of tyranny' precisely because 'all people' marvel at their 'courage and endurance'. By inspiring others to re-enact their resistance they create an implacable barrier to Antiochus's efforts, sending him finally on his way. Neither here nor at the passages where the brothers' obedience is called the ground of Antiochus's defeat (9.30; 11.24-25) is it suggested that the martyrs directly force Antiochus to leave. Rather, 1.11 and 18.5 make clear that the critical factor is the mimetic process by which others follow the martyrs' example.

It is odd that, with his penchant for martyrology and with the stress he lays on mimesis, the author has not seen fit to depict the Jerusalemites copying their models and dying obediently. His silence in this regard probably reflects a strident opposition to the entire Hasmonean legacy. According to *4 Maccabees*, warfare had nothing to do with saving Israel from Antiochus. Military and political leaders are read entirely out of this version of events. Instead, the author depicts pious, quietistic martyrs as heroes. He may well have been reluctant to broach the subject of exactly how Antiochus was driven out, fearing that questions might be raised about the role of Hasmonean combatants. Cautiously, he limits himself to a brief, summary remark such as 18.4-5. Nonetheless, his admonition at 7.8 shows what sort of response to hostile authority he advises, and, in turn, what is intended at 18.4-5.

In any case, it is clear that the vicarious effect of the martyrs' deaths can be appropriated mimetically even without having to re-enact literally their grisly end. As is true with *2 Maccabees* (see above, pp. 90-91), the re-enactment can be imaginative. At 14.9, the author admonishes his audience thus:

> Even now, we ourselves shudder as we hear of the tribulations of these young men; they not only saw what was happening, yes, not only heard the direct word of threat, but also bore the sufferings patiently, and in agonies of fire at that.

Here the author makes quite sure that his listeners/readers are imagining the deaths as vividly as possible. Through describing these deaths, he seeks to inspire obedience in his audience the way (he says) the martyrs' deaths inspired their contemporaries. This purpose accounts for the lingering, detailed description. By means of such mental re-enactment, the audience will benefit from the deaths. It will put itself in the martyrs' place, come to understand that it, too, could endure torment, and thus gain the courage to live, or, if necessary, to die obediently (cf. 18.1, the first direct exhortation to the audience, which is told to 'obey this law'). *4 Macc.* 7.9 supports this conclusion. There the author includes himself and his audience among those who benefit from Eleazar's actions.

> You, father, strengthened our loyalty to the law through your glorious endurance, and you did not abandon the holiness which you praised, but by your deeds you made your words of divine philosophy credible, ...

Eleazar's deeds lend credence to his philosophy, and prove that the latter can be followed. They strengthen 'loyalty to the law' because, when the audience hears Eleazar's story and mentally re-actualizes it, even faint-hearted individuals can dare to think 'He did it, so I can do it, too'. Indeed, the very nature of the story-telling process means that the audience has already done it imaginatively. (The role of story must also have been crucial in the inspiration of the martyrs' fellow-citizens; how else could they have heard about the executions?)

Obedience

That the martyrs' deaths are obedient has just been pointed out. Their obedience unto death is what makes them martyrs. It also allows them to claim a victory over Antiochus. Because they have remained obedient despite all his efforts, they have beaten him. In 8.2 the author says:

> For when the tyrant was conspicuously defeated in his first attempt, being unable to compel an aged man to eat defiling foods, then in violent rage he commanded that others of the Hebrew captives be brought, ...

But Antiochus is defeated by these other captives even more conspicuously. The second eldest calls out from his agony:

> Do you not think, you most savage tyrant, that you are being tortured more than I, as you see the arrogant design of your tyranny being defeated by our endurance for the sake of religion? (9.30)

Finally, the sixth brother taunts Antiochus as follows:

> We six boys have paralyzed your tyranny! Since you have not been able to persuade us to change our mind or to eat defiling foods, is not this your downfall? (11.24-25)

These passages are fairly clear and need little comment. The battle is joined over whether Antiochus can force the martyrs to disobey. If they disobey, he wins; if they remain obedient, he loses.

Military Context

The military context of the martyrs' deaths has been alluded to already. The deaths take place in the midst of a war between Antiochus and the majority of the Judaeans. At 7.4, Eleazar is compared to a city beseiged by machines of war.[1] Later in the same verse, it is said: 'he conquered his besiegers with the shield of his devout reason'.

At 9.23-24, the eldest brother tells his siblings:

> Imitate me, brothers, ... Do not leave your post in my struggle or renounce our courageous brotherhood. Fight the sacred and noble battle for religion.

---

1 Cf. A.J. Malherbe, 'Antisthenes and Odysseus, and Paul at War', *HTR* 76 (1983) 143-73.

At 13.16, the author exhorts his readers: 'Therefore let us put
on the full armor of self-control ...'[1] Finally, at 16.14, the
mother is addressed as 'soldier of God in the cause of religion'.
All these passages show that the military context has been
turned in a decidedly metaphysical direction. The martyrs
fight, not with iron or steel, but with devotion and obedience.
This sort of turn will be noted again with Paul and with the
Greco-Roman writers discussed in ch. 6.

Overcoming Physical Vulnerability

That the martyrs fight to gain victory over physical vulnerability is clear. *4 Maccabees* 1.1–3.18 provides a theoretical
debate on the conflict between 'devout reason' and feelings (*ta
pathe*).[2] The author names several feelings in 1.3-4, but the
way in which he shows the conflict being played out indicates
that, for him, emotion gains expression via bodily pain and
weakness. As he says in 1.7-9,

> I could prove to you from many and various examples that
> reason is dominant over the emotions, but I can demonstrate
> it best from the noble bravery of those who died for the sake of
> virtue, Eleazer and the seven brothers and their mother. All
> of these, by despising sufferings that bring death, demon-
> strated that reason controls the emotions.

The first martyr to die is Eleazer. The author meticulously
describes the tortures to which he is put, and sums up his presentation thus:

> the holy man died nobly in his tortures, and by reason he
> resisted even to the very tortures of death for the sake of the
> law.

The author concludes that what he has just described proves
his thesis: 'it is right for us to acknowledge the dominance of
reason when it masters even external agonies' (6.31).

Since the author set out to prove that reason is sovereign
over feeling, and since he concludes here at 6.31 that the

---

1 Cf. Malherbe, 'Antisthenes' 148-53.
2 Renehan, 'The Greek Philosophic Background' 223-38. I am translating *ta pathe*
   as 'feelings' because the latter combines emotive and physical connotations in a
   way that seems appropriate for *4 Maccabees*. 'Feelings' is, I think, a better translation than 'emotions', which the *Oxford Annotated Bible* uses.

mastery of reason over 'external agonies' proves the former's dominance, it seems clear that, for him, feeling is manifested most poignantly through one's body. Those who dedicate themselves to devout reason can control the 'feelings of the flesh' (*ta tēs sarkos pathē*) (7.18). This connection of feeling and flesh shows how the author conceives the former. The excruciating depictions of torture confirm this. The martyrs' inner resources are pitted against their outer, physical vulnerability to Antiochus.

Sacrificial Metaphors
Sacrifical metaphors are applied to the martyrs' deaths at *4 Maccabees* 6.28-29 and 17.21-22. But similarly to Paul (see Chapter 1), these metaphors are not as important as might be expected. Williams points out that the two passages just named

> cannot be separated radically from the objective historical effect of the martyrs' endurance unto death (17.20). In other words, the specifically religious categories used to express the effect and meaning of the martyrs' deaths in 6.28-29 (and 17.21-22) do not constitute an independent affirmation. Rather, they supplement the central assertion that the deaths were effective and beneficial for the nation in that Antiochus departed.[1]

The central affirmation regarding the deaths is that they were effective because of their obedience and exemplary nature. Because they possessed these two qualities, they caused Antiochus to leave. In addition to this central affirmation, the deaths can have sacrificial metaphors applied to them. This metaphorical status is shown by the 'as it were' in 17.21b and by the train of thought in the pericope (17.11-24). In 17.11-16, the author lauds the martyrs as contestants in a divine 'contest' (*agon*: a commonplace in philosophical debate).[2] Their endurance and refusal to disobey is marveled at by even Antiochus himself. Because of their endurance, they now stand at the heavenly throne. 'For Moses says, "All who are consecrated are under your hands" ' (17.19).

---

1 Williams, *Jesus' Death* 177-78.
2 Pfitzner, *Paul and the Agon Motif.*

Those who are thus consecrated

> are honoured, not only with this honor, but also by the fact
> that because of them our enemies did not rule over our
> nation, [and] the tyrant was punished . . . (17.20)

The author then proceeds to his sacrificial metaphor. But the
lines just paraphrased and quoted describe the historically
conceivable pattern by which the martyrs' obedience drives
out Antiochus. This pattern is fundamental. Sacrificial metaphors re-state and elaborate it.

A sequence similar to 17.11-24 is observed in 1.11. 'By their
endurance they conquered the tyrant, and thus their native
land was purified through them'. This verse does not employ
sacrificial metaphors, but 'purified' (cf. e.g. Lev. 11–16) is a
cultic term subservient to the consideration of exemplary,
obedient deaths. The fact that purification of the land occurs as
a result of the tyrant's defeat strongly suggests that the
impurity at issue was his presence as a foreign invader. When
he left because he could not force a populace inspired by the
martyrs' examples to abandon the Law, the land was thereby
purified.

At 6.29, as at 17.21-22, an interpretive operation is necessary for a martyrs' death to become sacrificial. Eleazer cries
out to God on behalf of the people: '*Make* my blood their purification, and *take* my life in exchange for theirs' (italics mine).
The effectiveness of Eleazer's death in cultic terms is thus
'dependent upon the way in which God regards it'.[1] *4 Macc.*
6.30 highlights not the cultic aspects of Eleazar's death, but the
martyrological ones:

> And after he said this, the holy man died nobly in his tor-
> tures, and by reason he resisted even to the very tortures of
> death for the sake of the law.

Context, and the author's decision about which aspects of
these deaths to develop, show that martyrological categories
are fundamental, though they are occasionally elaborated
through sacrificial metaphors.

---

1 Williams, *Jesus' Death* 177.

Conclusion

4 Maccabees has been shown to be, in a sense, like *2 Maccabees*, only more so. The mimetic mode of the martyrs' vicarious deaths is more pronounced, as is its availability via imaginative re-enactment in the story-telling process. The martyrs' obedience is highlighted as their means of gaining victory over Antiochus. The military context is harsher and more savage. And, the overcoming of physical vulnerability is given both a philosophical setting and a host of gruesome details. The Noble Death depicted in *2 Maccabees* is thus painted in even more vivid colors by is literary successor. *4 Maccabees* also adds a sacrificial aspect to the basic, martyrological pattern at two points.

The task now is to determine whether the Noble Death can be located in Paul, and whether he has similarly included a sacrificial aspect.

Paul

In this section, the same five components just traced will be isolated and analyzed in Paul. As before, the practice will be to proceed sequentially and discuss each component under its own heading.

Vicariousness

Perhaps the most significant passage in Paul for determining just how a believer 'gets in on' the vicarious effect of Jesus' death is Rom. 6.1-11.[1] There Paul addresses directly the issue of gaining benefit from Jesus' death. He states that Christians have died to sin by being baptized into Christ and his death (6.2-3). In the baptismal rite, Christians re-enact Jesus' death, destroy the sinful body, and gain release from slavery to sin (6.5-6).

Scholars have long recognized the importance of Rom. 6.1-11 in Pauline soteriology. For example, in trying to explicate the meaning of Jesus' death as a saving event, Bultmann writes that with Paul,

---

1 Cf. e.g. V.P. Furnish, *Theology and Ethics in Paul* (Nashville: Abingdon, 1968) 171.

> The essential thing ... is that ... the categories of cultic-
> juristic thinking are broken through: *Christ's death* is not
> merely a sacrifice which cancels the guilt of sin (i.e. the
> punishment contracted by sinning), but is also *the means of
> release from the powers of this age: Law, Sin, and Death.*[1]

Obviously, the next question is 'how Christ's death can have
such an effect'.[2] Or, in the phraseology used here: what is the
mode of vicariousness? This question, says Bultmann, 'finds an
answer in the statements in which *Paul describes Christ's
death in analogy with the death of a divinity of the mystery
religions'.*[3] Chapter 4 has shown that Bultmann's sense of
historical background was not entirely accurate here, but his
exegetical instincts were true. For from this point, he moves
directly to Romans 6. Bultmann understood that the latter
offers the best guide to solving the problem of how Jesus' death
confers benefit on others.

Käsemann, too, articulates the fundamental importance of
Romans 6 when he says in his exegesis of it that, in baptism,
Christ has gathered Christians into his death and his fate.[4]

Käsemann's connection of dying with Christ and baptism
may, indeed, be too close. The analysis of Gal. 2.20 in Chapter 2
noted that only in Romans 6 does Paul interpret baptism as
death and resurrection with Christ, and that Paul has no
difficulty speaking of dying with Christ in non-baptismal contexts. Still, Käsemann, like Bultmann, understands and
asserts the critical significance of this passage for compre-
hending the vicariousness of Jesus' death in Paul.

E.P. Sanders makes this significance even clearer when he
places Rom. 6.3-11 alongside Rom. 7.4; Gal. 2.19-20; 5.24; 6.14;
and Phil. 3.10-11. Like these other passages, but more fully,
Romans 6 shows that dying with Christ is the real means by
which the vicarious effect of Jesus' death is conveyed. Sanders
writes:

> We see in all these passages that the prime significance
> which the death of Christ has for Paul is not that it provides
> atonement for past transgressions ..., but that, by *sharing*

---

1 Bultmann, *Theology* 1.297-98.
2 Bultmann, *Theology* 1.298.
3 Bultmann, *Theology* 1.298.
4 Käsemann, *Romans* 165.

> in Christ's death, one dies to the *power* of sin or to the old
> aeon, with the result that one belongs to God. The *transfer* is
> not only from the uncleanness of idolatry and sexual
> immorality to cleanness and holiness, but from one lordship
> to another. The transfer takes place by *participation* in
> Christ's death.[1]

Although Sanders uses the term 'participation' here, the mimetic character of dying with Christ becomes evident when one realizes that it consists of a form of re-enactment.[2] The believer re-enacts Christ's death in his or her own life, just as the Israelites re-enacted the martyrs' deaths in their own lives (whether imaginatively or literally), and just as *4 Maccabees*' audience is called upon to re-enact such behaviour in its own life (again, whether imaginatively or literally).

The difference between Paul and *4 Maccabees* lies in Paul's mythologization of the mimetic pattern. One would not say that a person literally following the example of a martyr 'dies with' the latter, for the martyr is already dead. Now, Christ's crucifixion was a past event when the first believer was baptized, yet Paul speaks of dying with Christ. Paul seems to think that Christ's death is not limited by the constraints of temporality in the way other people's deaths are. It is in some sense a mythic event. Furthermore, the believer does not literally, physically cease to function (although, cf. Rom. 8.10). This fact suggests that, for Paul, 'death' is primarily a matter of being moved out of Sin's dominion (as Sanders indicates above). The enemy is mythic, not literal like Antiochus.

What Paul's mythologization achieves is a coalescence of the literal and the imaginative. In *4 Maccabees*, the martyrs gain a victory over Antiochus by resisting his compulsion even to the point of death—by dying literally (cf. *4 Macc.* 9.30; 11.24-25). Their fellow-citizens are then braced by their example—i.e. they imaginatively re-enact the martyrs' deaths. Finally, by following that example, and presumably

---

1 Sanders, *Paul and Palestinian Judaism* 467-68.
2 This is shown especially well by Rom. 6.5, where Paul uses the words 'a death like his'. After surveying the various exegetical options, F.A. Morgan, 'Romans 6, 5a: United to a Death like Christ's', *ETL* 59 (1983) 301, concludes that verse 5a can be paraphrased thus: 'If we have died to sin as Christ died...' Here the re-enactment of Christ's death by the believers stands clear.

suffering or dying themselves (cf. 18.4), they gain victory over Antiochus.

But in Paul, Jesus is the only one who dies literally. Believers re-enact that death by participating in the ritual of baptism. This corresponds closely to the imaginative re-enactment of those who hear the story of the martyrs' deaths, for the point of Rom. 6.32 is that the ritual of baptism *must* be seen in the context of the story about Jesus' death. This verse implies that the Christians in Rome are having difficulties because they have not properly interpreted the ritual in light of the story: Jesus' death was a death to sin; therefore, so is the 'death' of anyone who re-enacts it in baptism. But this last death is not the sort whereby the individual ceases to function physically. Believers' bodies may in some sense be 'dead', as Rom. 8.10 says, but they are still up and walking around.

Paul can say that believers who have seen their own fate in terms of Jesus' fate are dead because he has mythologized the concept of death. It no longer means 'cease to function physically', but 'leave the dominion of Sin'. Paul has taken the process which in *4 Maccabees* is preparatory to a literal death—imaginative re-enactment—and ascribed the sort of objective effects to it reserved in *4 Maccabees* for the literal. It is as if one of the martyrs' fellow-citizens or a listener/reader of *4 Maccabees* were able to share in the victory over Antiochus (9.30; 11.24-25) merely by digesting the story and seeing his or her own life in accordance with it.

Nonetheless, despite the mythic features which Paul utilizes, and despite his merging of the literal and imaginative levels, the resemblance of mimetic vicariousness in his work to what is found in *4 Maccabees* remains. This resemblance is the more striking since both types of mimetic vicariousness are joined with the other three elements of the Concept of the Noble Death, as well as with sacrificial metaphors.

Obedience

The above section has just pointed out that when believers re-enact Jesus' death in their own lives, they are freed from the rule of Sin. As Jesus 'died to sin' (Rom. 5.10) on the cross, so the believer dies to sin when he or she re-enacts Jesus' death. But why Jesus 'died to sin' in the first place—that is, how he was freed from sin—is not articulated. It is implied, however, in statements about Jesus' obedient death at Phil. 2.8 and Rom. 5.18-19. The former is traditional, as noted above (cf. Chapter 2). However, Paul has added a phrase of his own[1] and thus marked that point as especially important to him. He wishes to stress that it was precisely because of Jesus' obedience unto death that he was raised to a lordship. Obedience is what made his death special. Jesus dies obediently, is exalted, and is placed at the head of the new aeon.[2]

Rom. 5.18-19, too, places obedience at the hinge of the aeons. Rom. 5.12-21 elucidates Paul's aeon theology via an Adam-Christ typology. Verses 18-19 state:

> Then as one man's trespass led to condemnation for all men, so one man's act of righteousness leads to acquittal and life for all men. For as by one man's disobedience many were made sinners, so by one man's obedience many will be made righteous.

The 'act of righteousness' which 'leads to acquittal and life' is almost certainly the crucifixion. No other act of Christ's could be said by Paul to have such a salvific effect.[3] Because verses 18 and 19 are parallel, the crucifixion is very likely at issue in the latter, as well.[4] Just as Christ's 'act of righteousness' results in 'acquittal and life', so his 'obedience' makes many righteous. Therefore, if Christ's 'act of righteousness' denotes his crucifixion, and his 'obedience' has the same function as his 'act of right-eousness', then it follows that 'obedi-

---

1 F.W. Beare, *A Commentary on the Epistle to the Philippians* C; New York: Harper & Brothers, 1959) 85; Friedrich, 'Philipper' 110; Gnilka, *Philipperbrief* 137.

2 Cf. also Michaelis, *Philipper* 39; E. Peterson, *Frükirche, Judentum und Gnosis* (Rome, Freiburg, and Vienna: Herder, 1959) 121.

3 Cf. L.T. Johnson, 'Romans 3.21-26 and the Faith of Jesus', *CBQ* 44 (1982) 81, 89; S.K. Williams, 'The "Righteousness of God" in Romans', *JBL* 99 (1980) 277. The future tense of 5.19b need not militate against this interpretation. Paul elsewhere speaks of believers as already justified by Jesus' death, but here, directed by his Adam-Christ typology to a broader, eschatological vision (cf. 5.21), he seems to have something like 11.25 in mind. The future tense thus does not mean that no one has yet been justified—this would be nonsense for Paul—but that some portion of the 'many' is still outstanding.

4 Cf. R. Corriveau, *The Liturgy of Life* (Studia, Travaux de recherche 25; Brussels and Paris: Desclée de Brouwer; Montreal: Bellarmin, 1970) 172; Schlier, *Römerbrief* 175-76.

ence' denotes the crucifixion. A close association—not to say virtual identity—of obedience and death is thereby implied for Pauline soteriology.

Because Jesus was obedient even to the point of death, sin exercised no rule over him. He was and remained free from it.[1] So, when he died, he died to it as Rom. 5.10 indicates. Death put the cap on a sinless life and marked definitively Sin's inability to control Jesus' behaviour. When Jesus' sinless death is re-enacted, it thus frees the re-enactor from Sin's hold. This conclusion is supported by Rom. 6.17. You have been released from slavery to Sin, Paul tells his audience, and 'have become obedient from the heart to the standard of teaching to which you were committed'. Here the alternative to slavery under sin is obedience. The re-enactment of Jesus' death frees the believer from Sin and establishes him or her in righteousness. This indicates that the critical aspect of Jesus' death was its obedience. As Jesus' obedience kept him free from Sin's power, so also the believer who re-enacts that death is released from Sin and becomes obedient 'from the heart'.[2] This is how the vicariousness of Jesus' death is actualized.

2 Cor. 5.21 is another verse which very likely refers to Jesus' death.[3] To say that the sinless Jesus was made sin so that believers must become God's righteousness places Jesus' sinlessness at the beginning of a sequence which ends in salvation. God's making him sin would, of course, be unnecessary and illogical if he had already sinned. Now, because Romans 5 traces sin back to Adam's disobedience, not knowing sin must be tantamount to obedience. 2 Cor. 5.21 is therefore presenting Jesus' obedience as the ground of salvation. It, like Rom. 5.19, attributes the same function to Jesus' obedience as to his death. The logical conclusion is that this verse presupposes an obedient death as the basis for salvation.[4]

1 Williams, 'The "Righteousness of God" in Romans' 277.
2 Furnish, *Theology and Ethics* 172.
3 E. Dinkler, 'Die Verkündigung als eschatologisch-sakramentales Geschehen. Auslegung von 2 Kor 5.14-6.2', *Die Zeit Jesu* (eds. G. Bornkamm and K. Rahner; Freiburg, Basel, and Vienna: Herder, 1970) 181; O. Hofius, 'Erwägungen zur Gestalt und Herkunft des paulinischen Versöhnungsgedankens', *ZTK* 77 (1980) 188.
4 This procession of logic can be summarized as follows: 2 Cor. 5.21 indicates that Jesus' sinlessness leads to salvation; Romans 5 shows that sinlessness means

The situation is similar with Gal. 3.13. 'Christ redeemed us from the curse of the law, having become a curse for us—for it is written, "Cursed be every one who hangs on a tree" '. Here Paul is obviously referring to the crucifixion. But his use of the phrase 'having become' presumes Jesus' innocence. Jesus became a curse only at the crucifixion. He participated fully in the human condition (cf. Gal. 4.3-5), but without bringing the condemnatory force of the Law down upon himself—i.e. he lived obediently. Moreover, Jesus remained obedient even unto death, for according to Paul's scriptural explanation of the curse, it was attributed to Jesus because he hung upon a tree, not because he broke the Law.[1] Once again, Jesus' obedience stands at the starting point of events which culminate in salvation.

This discussion may not conclude without mention of Rom. 3.25. That verse is traditional,[2] but should still be looked at here.

The Greek phrase *dia pisteos* ('by faith') is generally taken as meaning the faith of believers. Williams, however, has noticed that the *dia* of the above phrase and the *en* translated as 'by' in 'by his blood' are structurally parallel to a *dia* and an *en* in the second half of 3.25 (the RSV roughly renders this *dia* as 'because' and translates this *en* as 'in').[3] According to such parallelism, *dia pisteos* depends on 'put forward', and *en* refers back to 'faith'. If one then takes the *en* as the 'instrumental dative of price',[4] one can translate 3.25a as follows: 'God "regarded" Christ crucified as a means of expiation by virtue of faith (i.e. his faith) at the cost of his blood'.[5]

Williams deals with the fact that nowhere else does the New Testament speak of Jesus' faith in two ways. First, he suggests

---

obedience; therefore, it can be said that according to 2 Cor. 5.21, Jesus' obedience leads to salvation; for Paul, Jesus' death is what brings salvation about; hence, 2 Cor. 5.21 must be talking about Jesus' obedient death.

1 Betz. *Galatians* 152; Schlier, *Galater* 140-41.
2 On the question of manuscript readings at this point, see Williams, *Jesus' Death* 41-42. On whether *dia pisteos* is a Pauline addition, see Williams, *Jesus' Death* 42-45.
3 Williams, *Jesus' Death* 46.
4 N. Turner in *Syntax*, vol. 3 of J.H. Moulton, *A Grammar of New Testament Greek* (Edinburgh: Clark, 1963) 253; cf. Williams, *Jesus' Death* 46.
5 Williams, *Jesus' Death* 47.

that a strict distinction between objective genitive and subjective genitive is not always necessary. At Rom. 3.21-22 and Gal. 3.22-25, Christ and faith are identified so closely that the ' "coming" of faith seems to be bound up with, dependent on, the coming of Christ. Thus he is the source of that faith which "comes" with him. In that sense it is "his" faith ..."Christ-faith" '.[1] Second, Williams refers to the Philippians hymn and Rom. 5.19, where the emphasis on Jesus' obedience provides a suitable context for interpreting 'faith' in Rom. 3.25 as meaning Jesus' faith/faithfulness.[2]

This last element brings us back to our beginning, of course. But the argument does not become circular. The point is simply that Rom. 3.25 can responsibly be interpreted in a fashion congruent with the Philippians hymn and Rom. 5.19.

Other recent exegetes agree with Williams' approach. P. Perkins, for instance, paraphrases Rom. 3.25-26 with a strong emphasis on Jesus' own faithfulness or obedience:

> God set forth (Jesus Christ) as a sin-offering—on account of his fidelity—at the cost of his blood; as a demonstration of his (=God's) righteousness, on account of his (=God) letting their (=Gentile) previous sins go unpunished due to God's restraint; as a sign of the righteousness of him who is righteous and makes righteous the person of Jesus' faith.[3]

L.T. Johnson writes that the 'close conjunction' in Greek of 'by faith' to 'expiation' and 'by his blood' suggests that the first phrase refers to the disposition of the one who was shedding his blood, viz. Jesus'.[4] Not surprisingly, he also feels that 'Rom. 5.18-19 explicates Rom. 3.21-26'.[5] R.B. Hays endorses Williams' interpretation of Rom. 3.25 as fitting into what he sees as the logic of Rom. 3.21-26.[6] He provides five reasons for considering the latter to be a reference to Jesus' faith: (1) Romans lacks any tendency to speak of Jesus as the object of faith;[7] (2)

---

1 Williams, *Jesus' Death* 48.
2 Williams, *Jesus' Death* 49.
3 P. Perkins, *Reading the New Testament* (New York and Ramsey, N.J.: Paulist Press, 1978) 150.
4 Johnson, 'Rom. 3.21-26' 79.
5 Johnson, 'Rom. 3.21-26' 81.
6 R.B. Hays, *The Faith of Jesus Christ* (SBLDS, 56; Chico, CA: Scholars Press, 1983) 170-74.
7 Hays, *The Faith* 170-71

the *pistis Iesou* (literally 'faith of Jesus') in 3.22 and 26 resembles the subjective genitives of 3.3; 4.12, and 4.16, while 3.21-26 offers no hint that Jesus is the object of faith;[1] (3) *ek pisteos Abraam* (literally 'of faith of Abraham'; Rom. 4.16) is parallel to *ek pisteos Iesou* (literally 'of faith of Jesus'; Rom 3.26);[2] (4) if 'faith *in* Jesus Christ' (Rom. 3.22) is an accurate translation, then 'for all who believe' makes the verse very redundant;[3] (5) the revelation of God's righteousness spoken of in 3.22 is much easier to conceive if Jesus is the possessor of faith rather than its object.[4]

All these passages, then, add up to a striking emphasis on Jesus' obedience as the most important aspect of his death. It is obedience which enables Jesus' death to become salvific.

Military Context

Paul frequently uses military metaphors in his letters.[5] Rom. 13.12; 2 Cor. 6.7; 10.4-5 and 1 Thess. 5.8 attest to this. It is not surprising, therefore, to find military language being used to explicate the meaning of Jesus' death. Paul's aeon theology, the importance of which has been stressed repeatedly, entails an essentially military conceptuality. The two aeons are pitted against each other as two kingdoms or dominions, with Jesus' death as the point at which one aeon gains ascendancy over the other.

This fact is particularly clear at 1 Thess. 5.10, which stands in a passage whose apocalyptic tone is set by verse 2: '... the day of the Lord will come like a thief in the night'. Paul exhorts his audience to don the 'breastplate' of faith and love and the 'helmet' of the hope of salvation (5.8). Believers will not fall under wrath (5.9) because Jesus' death enables them to live with him (5.10). The death has had the effect of shifting believers from the rule of wrath to that of life. There they will fight as warriors against the old dominion.

---

1 Hays, *The Faith* 171
2 Hays, *The Faith* 171. At this point Hays is close to the position of G. Howard, 'Romans 3.21-31 and the Inclusion of the Gentiles', *HTR* 63 (1970) 230-31. Howard, however, argues on theological rather than grammatical grounds.
3 Hays, *The Faith* 171-72.
4 Hays, *The Faith* 72.
5 Malherbe, 'Antisthenes' 143-73.

In Gal. 5.16-26, Paul designates the two aeons through speaking of two ways of living: by the Spirit or by the flesh. Those who are led by the Spirit are not under the Law (5.18); those who do the works of the flesh will not inherit the kingdom of God (5.21). The two ways are thus locked in a kind of combat: 'for these are opposed to each other' (5.17). Once again, the hinge between the aeons is the crucifixion. Those who belong to Christ 'have crucified the flesh' (5.24), and have thus been shifted out of the old aeon into the new. (Paul cautions against taking this shift for granted with his characteristic indicative/imperative in 5.25.)

1 Corinthians 10.14-22 engages Jesus' death as it is expressed in the eucharist. Those who participate in the latter are thereby bound to Jesus' lordship. They cannot then become partners with demons, as well, for there is an immutable hostility between these two rules. This hostility is so strong that Jesus could be moved to punish those who stray into that other realm (10.22).

The notion of two mortally opposed aeons occurs also in Romans 6. Paul begins the chapter by asking how those who died to sin can still live in it (6.2). The believer is thus not merely exhorted to stop sinning; the irrefutable facticity of his or her transference out of sin is affirmed, too. Paul does not ask how the believer can still practice sin, but how he or she can still live in it, as though it were a country or a kingdom. Like the passages just examined, Rom. 6 presents Jesus' death as the point at which transference takes place. It is better to say that Rom. 6 is about baptism as an expression of Jesus' death than to say that it is about baptism *per se*. Verse 3 shows this clearly: baptism *into Jesus' death* is what gives the rite its power. Thereby the believers die to one aeon and are proleptically raised to another (6.4-5, 8, 11).[1]

Paul also uses the language of hostile relations when he speaks of enslavement to one ruler or the other (6.6, 16-18, 20, 22). Sin dominates people like an evil tyrant (6.12-14). Those who have died with Christ escape its fatal suzerainty.[2]

---

1 Betz, *Galatians* 123. Cf. also 189.
2 Käsemann, *Romans* 168-69.

A number of exegetes have noted the military tone of the language by which Paul expresses his soteriology. Nygren, for instance, writes:

> The Christian has been 'brought from death to life'. Formerly his outpost was situated in enemy territory where death was in power. But now it has been captured and included in life's domain.[1]

Similarly, Schweizer compares this change in dominions to 'the victory of the allied forces in France' during World War II.[2]

Overcoming Physical Vulnerability

Paul employs Hellenistic language in Rom. 7.14-25.[3] This language most likely refers to a generalized, pre-Christian figure.[4] The meaning for Pauline anthropology is clear in any case: the power of sin, operating via the weakness of flesh, makes people incapable of implementing the good behaviour they wish in their inner selves to follow. They want to act in obedience to God's law, but they cannot do so. This represents a radicalized, apocalypticized version of the tension between inner and outer just observed in *4 Maccabees*: radicalized because it is *impossible*—rather than just difficult—to overcome physical vulnerability and conform with divine will, and apocalyptic because the flesh has been taken over by a mythic, guiding force. The person of Romans 7 thus cannot be placed in a strict parallel with the martyr/philosopher of *4 Maccabees*. If we consider the implications of Romans 7 for Pauline Christology, however, the match is seen to be much closer. For Christ lived and died obediently, even though he was in the flesh. This means that it was somehow possible for him to resist the constraints of sin working through the flesh. What is special about his death is the same thing that is special about the deaths of the martyrs, obedience. Paul's radicalization of the martyrological pattern means that, for him, Christ is the *only* one who died obediently. The pattern, however, remains. Just as the martyrs did not fall prey to the compulsion of Antiochus which was exercised upon their flesh, so Christ

---

1 Nygren, *Romans* 246.
2 Schweizer, 'Dying and Rising' 12.

must not have fallen prey to the compulsion of Sin which was exercised upon his flesh.

The position I have taken here is not an attempt to engage in pietistic psychology, merely an effort to understand the implications of Paul's anthropology for his Christology. In this light, it is difficult to see how the conclusions just drawn can be avoided.[1]

Sacrificial Metaphors

In Chapter 1, it was shown that sacrificial metaphors are, indeed, applied to Jesus' death in Paul. However, their status is secondary with respect to Paul's aeon theology.

Conclusion

It has been shown that Paul presents a radical, apocalyptic version of the pattern of mimetic vicariousness found in *4 Maccabees* and, less clearly, *2 Maccabees*. Paul views Jesus as the only one who has died an obedient death. He considers re-enactment of that death necessary for Christians but merges the literal and imaginative modes of re-enactment. This peculiarly Pauline mode is placed in an apocalyptic framework according to which two mythic realms or aeons battle with each other. Re-enacting Jesus' obedient death transfers a person from enslavement by an evil lord, Sin, to the rule of a benign lord, Jesus.

---

1 A supporting argument for this position lies in Rom. 6.5-6. Paul says that we have been united with Jesus in a death like his. The meaning of that death, for our part, is that 'our old self was crucified with him so that the sinful body might be destroyed, and we might no longer be enslaved to sin'. These terms are very close to what is found in Rom. 7.14-25. How could it be possible for our death, which is like Jesus' death, to entail the destruction of the body of sin and freedom from sin if Jesus' death itself did not involve some triumph over the body and the sin operating in it?

A possible objection to this is that Paul here uses 'body', while in 7.14-25 he uses 'flesh' But the parallelism of 'body' in 24b and 'flesh' in 25b shows the closeness of these two terms in this context. Another possible objection is that the 'old self' of 6.6 and the 'inmost self' 7.22 are not equal. This is true, but it does not tell against the argument being presented here. These two phrases are simply different ways Paul has of expressing the same essential dualism. That the crucifixion of the 'old man' still leaves a self (which can be exhorted) inside a mortal body subject to sin is shown by 6.12-13. Put simplistically, with the 'old self', the 'inner self' was completely bound by the sinful flesh; with the 'new self', the 'inner self' has a choice whether to be ruled by sin or by Christ.

General Conclusion

This chapter has demonstrated that *4 Maccabees'* account of the martyrs' deaths shares five components with Paul's account of Jesus' death.

The first component is vicariousness. By inspiring others to follow their example, i.e. to re-enact it either imaginatively or literally, the martyrs defeat Antiochus. Their deaths are set forth as having beneficial value in the author's own day, as well. He asks his audience to feel itself to be in the martyrs' place (cf. *4 Macc.* 14.9-10), and advocates following them literally, if need be (7.5). In this way the martyrs' deaths enable others to become free from Antiochus' (or, presumably, any tyrant's) rule. Paul, too, affirms that the believer must replicate the model's death, dying with Jesus in obedience and thereby gaining release from Sin's rule. *4 Maccabees* and Paul share a concern with the imaginative re-enactment of an obedient death. The former affirms a relatively straight-forward sort of identification. The latter presents a more mythic, mystical (to use Schweitzer's term[1]) sort of re-actualization. In each case, however, the basic pattern is the same.

The second component is obedience. The martyrs' deaths in *4 Maccabees* are martyrological precisely, and obviously, because they are obedient. Antiochus cannot break his victims' fidelity. Paul notes Jesus' obedience explicitly in Romans 5 and Philippians 2, while giving strong indications of it elsewhere.

The third component is a military context. *4 Maccabees'* military aspect is patent since the book describes part of the war between the Israelites and Antiochus Epiphanes. Paul's aeon theology involves a war between two mythic dominions vying for control of mankind.

The fourth component is overcoming physical vulnerability. In *4 Maccabees*, the inability of Antiochus to torture his captives into abandoning their 'devout reason' is several times referred to. In Paul, the anthropology of Romans 7 yields the Christological conclusion that only Jesus was able to resist the coercion of Sin operating through his flesh and to maintain the obedience desired by his inner man.

---

1 A. Schweitzer, *The Mysticism of Paul the Apostle* (trans. W. Montgomery; London: Black, 1931).

The last and least significant component is the use of sacrificial metaphors. In both cases, the language of cultic sacrifice does not express the real mechanism by which the deaths come to be beneficial for others. In *4 Maccabees*, these metaphors are marked as figurative, and in Paul, they are confined almost exclusively to traditional material.

Chapter 6

THE GRECO-ROMAN CONTEST
OF PAUL'S DOCTRINE OF SALVATION

Introduction

The previous chapter identified a cluster of components significant for *4 Maccabees'* interpretation of the martyrs' deaths and for Paul's interpretation of Jesus' death. The task of this chapter is to investigate the historical context of that cluster. *4 Maccabees'* strongly Hellenistic features and the above examination of possible Old Testament antecedents to Pauline soteriology (chs. 1–3) suggest that the literature of the Greco-Roman world should be considered here.

In that literature the Noble Death of the philosopher exhibits the same cluster of components that was found in *4 Maccabees* and Paul. The philosopher helps others by dying obedient to his philosophy, combatting and overcoming physical vulnerability. At times, this death can have sacrificial metaphors attached to it. In this chapter, investigation of the Noble Death will begin with Seneca and proceed to Epictetus, Silius Italicus, Plutarch, Tacitus, and Lucian.

Seneca

Seneca's Epistle 24 offers a convenient starting point for analysis of the Noble Death because it contains four of the five components just noted in a single, unified text. The sacrificial metaphor is missing, but that was identified as the least significant of the five components. (The sacrificial metaphor as it relates to the philosopher's death will be discussed later in this chapter.)

In Epistle 24, Seneca replies to his friend Lucilius, who has sought advice about his fears over a lawsuit. Seneca answers

that examples powerful enough to conquer even the strongest
fears are ready at hand. He then recounts the stories of Rutilius, Metellus, Socrates, Mucius, Cato, and Scipio. Three of
these (Socrates, Cato, and Scipio) died nobly, and the rest suffered likewise. As with *4 Maccabees* and Paul, the significant
features of these deaths will be discussed sequentially.

Vicariousness

The student of philosophy models himself after those who
have died nobly. By re-enacting imaginatively or literally the
deaths of those who have faced the worst with courage, he
gains freedom from all coercion. The examples of Noble Death
provide the basis on which the student gains his freedom, and
so can be said to have a vicarious effect. This is most clearly
seen in Seneca's comments on Socrates' death:

> Socrates in prison discoursed, and declined to flee when cer-
> tain persons gave him the opportunity; he remained there,
> in order to free mankind from the fear of two most grievous
> things, death and imprisonment.[1]

This passage is noteworthy on several grounds. First, Socrates is said to have remained in prison for the purpose of
benefitting mankind, this means that, in Seneca's mind, Socrates intended his incarceration and the execution which
ended it to be vicarious. Second, this behaviour is universal in
its consequences, offering benefit to mankind in general.
Third, it is powerful enough to remove the fear of something
as basic to human existence as death itself. Fourth, and most
importantly, it presupposes a mimetic response. Seneca obviously expects people to profit from Socrates' action. But the
only way they can do so is to re-enact it in their own lives.
Socrates is an example to be followed. That is why Seneca has
included him here. One must put oneself in his position,
adopting his attitude (obedience to philosophical principle even
at the cost of freedom and life) in light of one's own vulnerability and morality. This mimetic re-actualization or re-
enactment of the model's behaviour frees the follower from

---

1 Seneca, *Ad Lucilium Epistulae Morales* (LCL; trans. R.M. Gummere; Cambridge, Mass.: Harvard University Press; London: Heinemann, 1947) 24.4.

fear of captivity or death. Just as Socrates went to his end concerned only with acting rightly, so the follower who incorporates that pattern into his own life can do the same. In effect, imprisonment and death have no more hold over him, since he can now behave with no regard for them.

Seneca provides an excellent illustration of just how this process works when he discusses the death of Cato. On the night of the latter's suicide, he read 'Plato's book' with a sword by his pillow.

> He had provided these two requisites for his last moments,—
> the first, that he might have the will to die, and the second,
> that he might have the means ... Drawing the sword, ... he
> cried: 'Fortune, you have accomplished nothing by resisting
> all my endeavours ... Now, since the affairs of mankind are
> beyond hope, let Cato be withdrawn to safety'.[1]

Particular attention should be paid to the close link here between a kind of proclamation of the model's death (Socrates in 'Plato's book')[2] and Cato's re-enactment of it. Socrates' death takes place, it is set forth by Plato, and it is then used by followers like Cato. In a sense which is meaningful though not mythic as in Paul, Cato dies along with Socrates, utilizing his example as an enabling, empowering pattern by which to gain freedom from Fortune. Cato's suicide, performed in the appropriate way and at the appropriate time, renders him immune to Fortune's efforts.

The daeth of Cato, in turn, takes on its own vicarious aspect via proclamation by Seneca. The latter cautions Lucilius:

> I am not now heaping up these illustrations for the purpose
> of exercising my wit, but for the purpose of encouraging you
> to face that which is thought to be most terrible.[3]

Through pondering these examples and imaginatively re-enacting them, Lucilius will approach the level of a Socrates or a Cato. He will be able to lead his life with the courage and

---

1 Seneca, Ep. 24.6-7.
2 It might be objected that Cato was using 'Plato's book' merely for the arguments it presents, and not for the example of Socrates. One is hard-pressed, however, to separate these two, since the arguments of, say, the *Phaedo* (the dialogue most germane to Cato's situation and therefore the one probably in Seneca's mind) are presented by Socrates just before, and in light of, his martyrdom.
3 Seneca, Ep. 24.9.

integrity that they exhibited and, if necessary, to re-enact their deaths literally. He will thus become free from the fear of enemies or misfortunes of any kin.[1] Death and pain will no longer possess power over him.[2]

The imaginative re-enactment of a Noble Death was such an important issue in philosophical debate at this time that it had become a commonplace. Seneca remarks to Lucilius:

> I remember one day you were handling the well-known commonplace,—that we do not suddenly fall on death, but advance towards it by slight degrees; we die every day.[3]

Seneca invites Lucilius to consider in this regard a line of the latter's own poetry: 'Not single is the death which comes; the death/Which takes us off is but the last of all'.[4] The true philosopher should regard each passing moment as a sort of death, and thus follow the example of his models continually. He imaginatively re-enacts a Noble Death with every step he takes.

That pondering examples of the Noble Death was common at this time is suggested also by a rejoinder that Seneca makes to himself elsewhere. After mentioning Rutilius, Metellus, Socrates, and Mucius, he writes:

> 'Oh', say you, 'those stories have been droned to death in all the schools; pretty soon, when you reach the topic "On Despising Death", you will be telling me about Cato'.[5]

Seneca, of course, goes on to do precisely that. The point, however, is that the mimetically vicarious Noble Deaths of philosophical figures were virtual clichés, with which any schoolboy would have been familiar. The reason these deaths were repeated again and again in the schools is that they were judged to be helpful and beneficial to the students. In other words, they had a vicarious effect.

---

1   Seneca, Ep. 24.12.
2   Seneca, Ep. 24.14.
3   Seneca, Ep. 24.19.
4   Seneca, Ep. 24.21.
5   Seneca, Ep. 24.6.

Obedience

Obedience is an issue which is certainly present in Epistle 24 but the question of just what Seneca's exemplars are obedient to could have several answers: reason,[1] bravery,[2] wisdom.[3] The best answer, however, is probably philosophy. Having admonished Lucilius on how he should view death, Seneca says:

> Ponder these words which you have often heard and often uttered. Moreover, prove by the result whether that which you have heard and uttered is true. For there is a very disgraceful charge often brought against us,—that we deal with the words, and not with the deeds, of philosophy.[4]

One must remain obedient to one's philosophy—it is this simple but fundamental rule that Seneca is stressing. A philosopher who speaks the words of his philosophy but does not behave according to them is no philosopher at all. The examples of Socrates and Cato show men who remained obedient to philosophical principle even at the cost of their lives.

Military Context

A military context is provided for Epistle 24 by reference to the general Scipio (Gnaeus Pompeius' father-in-law)[5] and to Cato's plight at the end of the civil war between Caesar and Pompey.[6] It should be noted, however, that both of these figures are presented as examples of philosophical virtue rather than martial valor. Neither actually dies in battle. Scipio, seeing his ship fall into the enemy's hands, skewers himself with a sword. Asked the whereabouts of the commander, he responds: 'All is well with the commander'.[7] With this statement, says Seneca, he raises himself to the stature of his forebears who died in Africa. 'It was a great deed to conquer Carthage, but a greater deed to conquer death'.[8] Thus, it is the

---

1 Cf. Seneca, Ep. 24.24.
2 Cf. Seneca, Ep. 24.25.
3 Cf. Seneca, Ep. 24.25.
4 Seneca, Ep. 24.15; adapted from Gummere's translation.
5 Seneca, Ep. 24.9-10.
6 Seneca, Ep. 24.7.
7 Seneca, Ep. 24.9.
8 Seneca, Ep. 24.10.

nobility of Scipio's death and the appropriate comment there-
on which is the focus here, not Scipio's (dubious) prowess as a
general. Nonetheless, the military setting remains significant,
for Scipio is a combatant in an even greater battle than his
ancestors fought, namely, the battle with death. By dying
nobly, he can be said to have defeated death, showing that it
had no compelling power over him.

Cato's situation is similar. The forces of Pompey, with
whom he has fought, have been beaten. As mentioned, he cries
at the end: 'Fortune, you have accomplished nothing by
resisting all my endeavours'.[1]

Like Scipio's combat, Cato's literal, military exercise is
translated into a grander, mythic battle. He addresses neither
Caesar, his enemy, nor Pompey, his general, but the mythic
figure of Fortune. In both cases the military tone retains its
importance, but is turned in a decidedly mythological direction.[2] What determines victory is no longer strategy or num-
bers, but a dedication to philosophical principle. Similarly, the
foe is no longer another soldier, but a mythologized, personified
abstraction such as Death or Fortune.

Overcoming Physical Vulnerability
At several points, Seneca articulates the philosopher's attitude
towards death, pain, and the body in dualistically oriented
terms. In a passage that recalls portions of *4 Maccabees*, he
writes:

> why dost thou hold up before my eyes swords, fires and a
> throng of executioners raging about thee? Take away all that
> vain show, behind which thou lurkest and scarest fools! Ah!
> It is nought but Death, whom only yesterday a man-servant
> of mine and a maid-servant did despise! Why dost thou again
> unfold and spread before me, with all that great display, the
> whip and the rack? Why are those engines of torture made
> ready, one for each several member of the body, and all the
> other innumerable machines for tearing a man apart piece-

---

1 Seneca, Ep. 24.7.
2 This same turn occurs in the example of Mucius. Of him, Seneca says that 'Here
   was a man of no learning, not primed to face death and pain by any words of
   wisdom, and equipped only with the courage of a soldier ...' Ep. 24.5. The
   implication is that Mucius, though only a fighting man, raised himself to the
   level of one trained by learning and wisdom, i.e. a philosopher.

meal? Away with all such stuff, which makes us numb with terror! And thou, silence the groans, the cries, and the bitter shrieks torn out of the victim as he is torn on the rack! Forsooth it is naught but Pain, scorned by yonder gout-ridden wretch, endured by yonder dyspeptic in the midst of his dainties, borne bravely by the girl in travail.[1]

A paragraph later, Seneca urges Lucilius to 'Say to yourself that our petty bodies are mortal and frail ...'[2] In the paragraph after that, Seneca writes: 'Behold this clogging burden of a body, to which nature has fettered me!'[3] Physical weakness must continually be battled and overcome in favor of philosophical principle.

Other instances of the Noble Death are not hard to find in the works of Seneca. (Due to the brevity of the remaining treatments of Seneca's texts, I will dispense with the customary sub-headings. The aspects of the Noble Death will nevertheless be taken up in the customary sequence.)

In 'De Providentia', Seneca refers to the death of Regulus. The latter was a consul captured by the Carthaginians in the First Punic War. His captors sent him back to Rome temporarily with the understanding that he would recommend favorable peace terms for them. Upon arrival, he denounced these terms to the Senate, but honoring his promise to return, he went back to Carthage and was tortured to death. Concerning him, Seneca asks:

> What injury did Fortuna do to him beacuse she made a pattern (*documentum*) of loyalty, a pattern (*documentum*) of endurance? Nails pierce his skin, and wherever he rests his wearied body he lies upon a wound; his eyes are stark in eternal sleeplessness. But the greater his torture is, the greater shall be his glory.[4]

By calling Regulus a pattern, Seneca notes the role his manner of death plays in vicariously enabling others to achieve a like measure of virtue and glory. His death provides a model of the loyalty and endurance which any student of philosophy

---

1 Seneca, Ep. 24.14; slightly adapted from Gummere's translation.
2 Seneca, Ep. 24.16.
3 Seneca, Ep. 24.17. Cp. Rom. 7.24.
4 Seneca, 'De Providentia', *Moral Essays* (LCL; trans. J.W. Basore; London: Heinemann; New York: Putnam, 1928) 3.9.

might be expected to have. By following his example mentally and being prepared to follow it literally, such a student can gain a similar degree of strength and dedication.

So seriously does Seneca take the mimetic attraction of Regulus that he contrasts him with the rich, jaded Maecenas and remarks:

> Surely the human race has not come so completely under the sway of vice as to cause a doubt whether, if Fate should give the choice, more men would rather be born a Regulus than a Maecenas.[1]

Similarly, one should envy Socrates and his hemlock more than those served the finest wines in the most elaborate fashion.[2]

The theme of obedience is manifested here by Regulus' fidelity to his promise. He pledged that he would return to the Carthaginians, and he obeyed that pledge. He paid for his obedience with his life.

A military context is readily apparent here, since Regulus is the Carthaginians' prisoner of war. Particular attention should be paid, however, to the fact that the above passage contains another mythologization of the military context. Here, Regulus is effectively locked in combat with Fortune. Seneca goes on to suggest that Fortune does not really harm Regulus because the ills she inflicts bring him glory. Nevertheless, Regulus' immediate opponent here is the personified abstraction Fortune, not the Carthaginians.

Readily apparent also in this passage is the overcoming of physical vulnerability. Regulus dies 'suffering hardship for the sake of right'. The fortitude with which he endures horrible tortures is precisely what brings him glory.

Elsewhere in 'On Providence', Seneca states that Fortune:

> Seeks out the bravest men to match with her; some she passes by in disdain. Those that are most stubborn and unbending she assails, men against whom she may exert all her strength. Mucius she tries by fire, Fabricius by poverty, Rutilius by exile, Regulus by torture, Socrates by poison, Cato

---

1 Seneca, Prov. 3.11.
2 Seneca, Prov. 3.13.

by death. It is only evil fortune that discovers a great exemplar (*exemplum*).[1]

By dying in an exemplary manner, these men offer vicarious benefit to others. The latter can imitate the models' deaths, become as 'stubborn and unbending' (i.e. as obedient to what is right) as they were, and thereby gain victory in their own military context. That is, they can be matched with Fortune and beat her. Even though Fortune may threaten one's physical vulnerability with fire, poverty, exile, torture, poison, and even death, she can be beaten. The exemplars have shown this. These men and their imitators can truly echo Paul's question, 'O death, where is thy victory?' (1 Cor. 15.55), even if they cannot share his theology.

Later in 'De Providentia', Seneca depicts Cato's opponent not as Fortune, but as Nature. He says that 'Nature' chose Cato 'to be the one with whom her dread power should clash'.[2] Despite this change in opponents from Fortune to Nature, the exemplary function of Cato's death remains the same. Nature proclaims that she has subjected Cato to the hatred of the first triumvirate, a humiliating defeat in his run for office, the rigors of civil war, and finally death by his own hand. 'And what shall I gain thereby?' she asks. 'That all may know that these things of which I deemed Cato worthy are not real ills'.[3] The purpose of Cato's suffering and death is thus to extend vicarious benefit to others. Through his example, all may come to understand the truth about life. Because Cato's obedience to the right remained unbroken by any of the salvos which Nature launched against him, he serves as a model of instruction for all men. Armed with such instruction, others may follow his example and become effectively immune to Nature's assaults, for they will know that such vicissitudes are 'not real ills'. They, too, will have overcome the vulnerability to which flesh is heir.

Later still in 'De Providentia', a passage occurs which is similar to the one just examined, but even more succinct. Seneca asks why God makes good men prey to the loss of property

---

1 Seneca, Prov. 3.4.
2 Seneca, Prov. 3.14.
3 Seneca, Prov. 3.14.

and sons, to exile, and to death. The answer: 'It is that they may teach others to endure them; they were born to be a pattern'.[1] Good men, in effect, are born to suffer and die on others' behalf. Seneca here goes so far as to say that that is the purpose of their existence. One gains benefit from their pattern of obedience by incorporating it into one's own life. One can thereby learn to conquer hardship and death through overcoming the physical vulnerability on which they prey.[2]

In Epistle 67, Seneca presents yet another discussion of the Noble Death:

> Clothe yourself with a hero's courage, and withdraw for a little space from the opinions of the common man. Form a proper conception of the image of virtue, a thing of exceeding beauty and grandeur; this image is not to be worshipped by us with incense or garlands, but with sweat and blood. Behold Marcus Cato, laying upon that hallowed breast his unspotted hands, and tearing apart the wounds which had not gone deep enough to kill him![3]

Seneca urges his reader to become 'clothed' in heroic courage (cf. Rom. 13.14), and to conceive properly the image of virtue.

---

1 Seneca, Prov. 6.3.
2 Further material on obedience, military context, and overcoming physical vulnerability in 'De Providentia' is as follows:

Obedience. At 2.4, Seneca states that 'not what you endure, but how you endure, is important'. That is, the character of one's obedience to the right even in the face of suffering is what matters. Similarly, Cato's failed suicide attempt is attributed to the gods' desire to see his virtue prove itself true more than once: 'His virtue was held in check and called back that it might display itself in a harder role; for to seek death needs not so great a soul as to reseek it'. (2.12) At 3.1, Seneca affirms that good men should be willing to suffer. At 3.9, Seneca asks regarding Regulus: 'Would you like to know how little he regrets that he rated virtue at such a price? Make him whole again and send him back to the senate; he will express the same opinion'.

Military Context. At 4.4-9, Seneca compares the great man to a soldier and a gladiator. At 5.1, the military motif is combined with vicariousness: 'Consider, too, that it is for the common good to have the best men become soldiers, so to speak, and do service. It is God's purpose, and the wise man's as well, to show that those things which the ordinary man desires and those which he dreads are really neither goods nor evils'.

Overcoming Physical Vulnerability. At 6.1, Seneca writes that the good man despises externals. God tells good men 'your goods are directed inward'. The good man should scorn Fortune, since God has given her no weapon that can touch the soul, 6.6.
3 Seneca, Ep. 67.12.

Indeed, this image is to be worshipped. How? Not with mere sacramental externals, but with 'sweat and blood'. Here we arrive at the mimetic crux of the issue. Gaining benefit from the model is done by imitating an obedient death, for the next thing Seneca says is 'Behold Marcus Cato' and his death. Cato demonstrated his worshipful obedience to the image of virtue with 'sweat and blood' (i.e. an obedient death). Any who would gain benefit by being clothed in his sort of courage should mentally re-enact his example and be prepared to do the same.

A military context is not explicitly stressed here, but any reader would have remembered the circumstances of Cato's death. In addition, the sentence just before the quote mentions Regulus, and the paragraph following the quote refers to Attalus, who said 'I should prefer that Fortune keep me in her camp rather than in the lap of luxury'.[1] Here is seen once again the motif of battle with the mythic, personified abstraction Fortune.

Overcoming physical vulnerability is exhibited by the example of Cato's hard-won, painful suicide.

A further illustration of the Noble Death is found in Seneca's Epistle 98.12-14. He says that of all the horrific experiences possible, 'none is insuperable'. He then lists his exemplars, Mucius, Regulus, Socrates, Rutilius, and Cato, and concludes: 'therefore, let us also overcome something'. We, too, should act courageously; we, too, should be among the examplars. This can be done 'if only we purify our souls and follow Nature'. Then we will be able 'to endure pain, in whatever form it attacks our bodies, and say to Fortune: "You have to deal with a *man*; seek someone whom you can conquer" '.

This passage exhibits clearly the components of vicariousness (the exemplars provide the standard which allows us to overcome, gain courage, and become examplars ourselves), obedience (to Nature, in this case), a military context (here the battle with Fortuna), and overcoming physical vulnerability (we beat Fortune by withstanding the assaults of pain).

---

1 Seneca, Ep. 67.15.

Summary
Seneca thus offers a number of instances of the Noble Death. Four of the five components isolated in *4 Maccabees* and Paul are amply documented. Indeed, Seneca notes that the Noble Death had become a commonplace so often discussed that schoolboys were sick of hearing about it.

The fifth component isolated in Chapter 5, sacrificial metaphor, was seen in that chapter to be ancillary. It will be treated later in this chapter in a section of its own.

Epictetus

Examples of the philosopher's Noble Death are found also in Epictetus. An especially good one is the following which concerns Diogenes and needs to be quoted at length:

> But I can show you a free man, so that you will never again have to look for an example. Diogenes was free. How did that come? It was not because he was born of free parents, for he was not, but because he himself was free, because he had cast off all the handles of slavery, and there was no way in which a person could get close and lay hold of him to enslave him. Everything he had was easily loosed, everthing was merely tied on. If you had laid hold of his property, he would have let it go rather than follow you for its sake; if you had laid hold of his leg, he would have let his leg go; if of his whole paltry body, his whole paltry body; and so also his kindred, friends, and country. He knew the source from which he had received them, and from whom, and upon what conditions. His true ancestors, indeed, the gods, and his real Country he would never have abandoned, nor would he have suffered another to yield them more obedience and submission, nor could any other man have died more cheerfully for his Country. For it was never his wont to seek to *appear* to do anything in behalf of the Universe, but he bore in mind that everything which has come into being has its source there, and is done on behalf of that country, and is entrusted to us by Him who governs it.[1]

---

1 Epictetus, 4.1.152-55.

Vicariousness
Diogenes would have died cheerfully on behalf of his true country, which was the Universe. The assertion that the Universe is Diogenes' country raises the question of just how his death is vicarious. Since the Universe is not literally a country or nation-state, Diogenes cannot die on its behalf the way a soldier would die for his country. He must die for it in a more figurative sense. This conclusion is supported by the passage's first sentence, in which Epictetus announces his purpose in discussing Diogenes: '... I can show you a free man, so that you will never again have to look for an example'. Diogenes' death is presented as the capstone, the logical conclusion of his devotion to freedom. He was always ready to give up all for the sake of others. This death forms the ultimate part of Diogenes' status as an 'example' (*Paradeigma*!). It shows as starkly as possible the path which all virtuous people can walk to freedom.

Obedience
The theme of obedience is explicit here. Diogenes would allow no one to be more obedient (*mallon ... hypakouein*) to the gods than he. Immediately after this statement, Epictetus writes that no one would have died more cheerfully for his 'Country'. Diogenes' death is the extreme manifestation of his obedience.

Military Context
A military context is indicated by Diogenes' willingness to die for his 'Country'. Even though this 'Country' is metaphorical, it can still be seen to have a relationship to literal nations. It stands counterposed to them, and the tension between the two can easily reach the point of violence—if not open warfare. One sentence after the quotation, Diogenes is told that he is permitted 'to converse as you please with the king of the Persians and with Archidamus, the king of the Lacedaemonians'. Others cannot do so because they are afraid of what might happen to them. Diogenes, however, is not afraid. Even the killing of his 'paltry body' is something he would suffer cheerfully in obedience to the gods and on behalf of his 'Country'. He, as the representative of one polity, confronts representatives of other polities (e.g. kings) fearlessly. Thus, Epic-

tetus' comments on Diogenes presuppose a sort of battle between two realms, with the philosopher appearing as a soldier on the front lines, liable to capture and death. Elsewhere, Epictetus explicitly places the philosopher in a military context.[1]

Overcoming Physical Vulnerability
Diogenes' power to overcome physical vulnerability is enunciated by the statement that 'if you had laid hold of his leg, he would have let his leg go; if of his whole paltry body, his whole paltry body'. Diogenes is prepared at any time to allow his physical being to be destroyed in favor of preserving his philosophical integrity and obedience to the gods.

Epictetus' treatment of Socrates, which follows directly on his treatment of Diogenes, is similar in many ways. Epictetus is concerned that his readers might think the example of Diogenes shows that only a man unencumbered by wordly cares can be truly free. So, he offers the example of Socrates, too:

> ... take Socrates and observe a man who had a wife and little children, but regarded them as not his own, who had a country, as far as it was his duty, and in the way in which it was his duty, and friends, and kinsmen, one and all subject to the law and to obedience to the law. That is why, when it was his duty to serve as a soldier, he was the first to leave home, and ran the risks of battle most ungrudgingly; and when he was sent by the Tyrants to fetch Leon, because he regarded it as disgraceful, he never deliberated about the matter at all, although he knew that he would have to die, if it so chanced. And what difference did it make to him? For there was something else that he wished to preserve; not his paltry flesh, but the man of honour, the man of reverence, that he was.[2]

Vicariousness
That this death includes a definite, vicarious aspect is shown by Epictetus' further comments on Socrates. If we had been in the latter's place, says Epictetus, we would have rationalized

---

1   Cf. *inter alia*, 3.22.19-26.
2   Epictetus, 4.1.159-161.

escape by pointing out that, alive, we could still be of use to people. But

> ... If we were useful to men by living, should we not have done much more good to men by dying when we ought, and as we ought? And now that Socrates is dead the memory of him is no less useful to men, nay, is perhaps even more useful, than what he did or said while he still lived.[1]

How is this memory useful? Because it leaves a paradigm which provides others the way to freedom. They can remember what Socrates did and gain strength from it, thus mentally re-enacting his death. In the extreme, they can follow it literally. Immediately after the passage just quoted, Epictetus makes the process of mimetic re-enactment of the model's death very clear. The reader should study the deeds of Diogenes and Socrates, and should:

> look at these examples, if you wish to be free, if you desire the thing itself in proportion to its value. And what wonder is there if you buy something so great at the price of things so many and so great? For the sake of what is called freedom some men hang themselves, others leap over precipices, sometimes whole cities perish; for true freedom, which cannot be plotted against and is secure, will you not yield up to God, at His demand, what He has given? Will you not, as Plato says, study not merely to die, but even to be tortured on the rack, and to go into exile, and to be severely flogged, and, in a word, to give up everything that is not your own?[2]

The deaths of men like Diogenes and Socrates provide paradigms for others. These paradigms can then be followed by those who would thereby gain freedom. When one studies how to die and how to give up everything not one's own, these paradigmatic deaths are *what* one studies! They are re-enacted in the mind and, if necessary, in the flesh. By doing so, one gains benefit.

Obedience

Epictetus mentions that Socrates, like his fellow-citizens, was obedient to the law, suggests that Socrates would no more have

---

1 Epictetus, 4.1.168-69.
2 Epictetus, 4.1.170-72.

disobeyed as a philosopher than as a soldier (cf. Plato's *Apology* 1.28B-29A), and asserts that Socrates' primary consideration was to maintain his honor and reverence. If Socrates' obedience to what he believes right gets him killed (as it nearly did under the Tyrants), then what matter? Obedience must be preserved, even at the cost of one's life.

When Epictetus asks 'will you not yield up to God, at His demand, what He has given?' he echoes what he had said earlier about Diogenes. The latter knew whence he had received everything. So, the true philosopher should readily follow God's order, if He requires his gifts (even life itself) back again. One should 'study' how to die in order to be prepared to follow God's orders obediently.

Epictetus coordinates Socrates' risking his life in battle with his risking his life to preserve his status as an obedient, faithful individual (*pistos*). This parallel is striking in that it presents a military context and highlights Socrates' willingness to die obediently and with no thought for his 'paltry body'. Socrates is a good soldier both of Athens and of God.

Overcoming Physical Vulnerability
Epictetus' remarks on studying not merely to die, but how to die in agonizing ways, underlines the role played here by overcoming physical vulnerability. Considerations of the flesh must not be allowed to deter the philosopher from his obedience.

Socrates and Diogenes are models of the Noble Death later in Epictetus' discourses, as well. (Due to the brevity of the remaining treatments of Epictetus' texts, sub-headings will again be dispensed with.) Why, Epictetus asks, should one worry about the tyrant?

> He is not Socrates, is he, or Diogenes, so that his praise should be a proof of what I am? I have not been ambitious to imitate his character, have I? Nay, but acting as one who keeps the game going, I come to him and serve him so long as he commands me to do nothing foolish or unseemly. If, however, he says, 'Go and bring Leon of Salamis'. I reply, 'Try to get someone else, for I am not playing any longer'. 'Take him off to prison', says the tyrant about me. 'I follow, because that is part of the game'. 'But your head will be taken

off. And does the tyrant's head always stay in its place, and
the heads of you who obey him? 'But you will be thrown out
unburied'. If the corpse is I, then I shall be thrown out; but if
I am something different from the corpse, speak with more
discrimination, as the fact is, and do not try to terrify me.[1]

Here again the themes of mimesis and the philosopher's death
appear. The speaker is anxious to imitate the character of his
models. This may, of course, involve risking death, as Socrates
did when he refused to arrest Leon of Salamis. It may even
involve death itself. But it will gain one the benefit of becoming
free from a tyrant's attempts to terrify. One will gain the goal
of resembling the character of the models. This is achieved by
mentally re-enacting the models' deaths. The speaker imag-
ines himself after death, with his corpse, a mere husk, thrown
out. By seeing himself going through the same process of
remaining obedient to virtue despite death, he gains the same
freedom Socrates and Diogenes had.

A military context is not explicit here, but clearly the philosopher is locked in a battle with the wordly authorities that try
to coerce him through making him suffer and die. The philosopher, however, overcomes his physical vulnerability[2] and
maintains obedience even to death.

The philosopher's death as paradigm is set forth yet again in
Epictetus when the interlocuter asks the speaker 'What will
you make of death?' The answer: 'Why, what else but make it
your glory, or an opportunity to show in deed thereby what
sort of person a man is who follows the will of nature'.[3] Death
is a philosopher's best opportunity to exhibit the worth of himself and his philosophy, thus recommending the former as a
pattern for others to copy and the latter as a way of life to be
adopted. By remaining obedient to Nature even at the cost of
his life, the philosopher shows others a pattern they can re-
enact mentally or, if necessary, literally.

---

1 Epictetus, 4.7.29-31.
2 Epictetus' insinuation that his corpse is not himself echoes Diogenes Laertius
  6.79 and Plato, *Phaedo* 115C-E.
3 Epictetus, 3.20.13.

Silius Italicus

The story of Regulus, encountered above in the discussion of Seneca, is given a lengthy treatment by Silius Italicus (26 AD–101 AD). Typically, his Noble Death is held up as an example to be re-enacted and lived up to. An old comrade-in-arms of Regulus says to the hero's son:

> Nor could I now essay to tell you how the people of Carthage behaved with the cruelty of wild beasts, if mankind had ever seen in any part of the world a nobler example than was set by the splendid courage of your father. I am ashamed to complain of tortures which I saw him endure with cheerfulness. You too, dear youth, must still think yourself worthy of such a glorious descent, and check those starting tears.[1]

Vicariousness
The old veteran hesitates to tell the gruesome story of Regulus' demise, but feels compelled to do so in order that its benefit can be made accessible. His own character has been raised by Regulus'. Whenever he feels tortured, he puts himself in the place of his commander, who bore the worst tortures cheerfully. The old man counsels Regulus' son to follow his father's example, too, and measure up to the glory of his deeds. Imaginative re-enactment of his death will benefit them.

Obedience
Silius leaves no doubt that Regulus' death was an obedient one. Arriving in the Senate from Carthage he gave this declamation:

> O ruler of the universe, source of justice and truth; and O Loyalty, no less divine to me, and Juno of Tyre, ye gods whom I invoked to witness my oath that I would return, if I am permitted to speak words that befit me, and by my voice to protect the hearths of Rome, not unwillingly shall I go back to Carthage, keeping my promise to return and enduring the prescribed penalty.[2]

---

1 Silius Italicus, *Punica* (LCL; trans J.D. Duff; Cambridge, Mass.: Harvard University Press; London: Heinemann, 1949) 6.531-38.
2 Silius Italicus, 6.466-72.

In obedience to justice and truth, and calling on Loyalty (*Fides*), Regulus returns to Carthage. His old comrade says:

> His laurels will be green throughout the ages, as long as unstained Loyalty keeps her seat in heaven and on earth and will last as long as virtue's name is worshipped.[1]

A military context is obvious here. Regulus was a general captured in war and sent home to urge peace terms favourable to the Carthaginians. It should be noted that there is an indication here of the same sort of mythologization of the military context which was observed in Seneca. When Regulus is taken from prison to the Carthaginian ship on which he will sail to Rome, the scene is portrayed almost as if he were marching in Fortune's triumph.

> ... then all the people hastened to the shore—women and boys and old men. Through the midst of the crowd and before their unfriendly eyes Regulus was brought along by Fortune, for them to look at.[2]

When this statement is coupled with those just quoted regarding Regulus' devotion to Loyalty, the situation begins to look like a battle between two mythic powers. Regulus is devoted to one power and dies on its behalf, having been killed but not truly beaten by the other power. Though he is exhibited as a captive of Fortune, his unbending dedication to Loyalty gives him the final victory.

Overcoming Physical Vulnerability
The theme of overcoming physical vulnerability is inherent in Regulus' determined forebearance of physical suffering. His comrade says:

> To contend with pressing evils—squalid attire and meagre fare and a hard bed—this he thought more glorious than to win a battle; and he held it a nobler thing to conquer by endurance than to avoid it by precaution.[3]

---

1 Silius Italicus, 6.546-49.
2 Silius Italicus, 6.366-68.
3 Silius Italicus, 6.373-76.

Regulus' expression remained unchanged even during torture.[1] '... he remained obdurate against grief and never bowed his neck to pain'.[2] Finally, of course, he endured cheerfully the awful tortures which the Carthaginians inflicted on him.[3]

Plutarch

Plutarch addresses the Noble Death in an essay titled 'On Tranquility of Mind'. Advising his readers on how to get and maintain such tranquility, he says:

> Therefore we should not altogether debase and depreciate Nature in the belief that she has nothing strong, stable, and beyond the reach of Fortune, but, on the contrary, since we know that the corrupt and perishable part of man wherein he lies open to Fortune is small, and that we ourselves are masters of the better part, in which the greatest of our blessings are situated—right opinions and knowledge and the exercise of reason terminating in the acquisition of virtue, all of which have their being inalienable and indestructible—knowing all this, we should face the future undaunted and confident and say to Fortune what Socrates, when he was supposed to be replying to his accusers, was really saying to the jury, 'Anytus and Maletus are able to take away my life, but they cannot hurt me'. Fortune, in fact, can encompass us with sickness, take away our possessions, slander us to people or despot; but she cannot make the good and valiant and high-souled man base or cowardly, mean, ignoble, or envious, nor can she deprive us of that disposition, the constant presence of which is of more help in facing life than is a pilot in facing the sea.[4]

Vicariousness

Vicariousness is shown here by the admonition to follow Socrates in his rejoinder to the jury. This rejoinder expresses Socrates' willingness to die bravely. When we face hard times, we should cleave to Socrates' example (having mentally re-

---

1 Silius Italicus, 6.388.
2 Silius Italicus, 6.413-14.
3 Silius Italicus, 6.536.
4 Plutarch, *Moralia* (LCL; trans. W.C. Helmbold; Cambridge, Mass.: Harvard University Press; London: Heinemann, 1939) 475D-475F.

enacted it and thus having shaped our lives in accordance with it). His courage in the face of impending death can become our own.

The theme of dying as the role model died becomes stronger when Plutarch develops the idea (stated in the last sentence of the quotation) of a pilot and the sea. The true philosopher can ride out harsh storms, but if he is entirely shipwrecked, then 'he may swim away from his body, as from a leaky boat'.[1] After this, Plutarch states directly what he feels to be the heart of the matter: 'For it is the fear of death ... which makes the fool dependent on his body ...'[2]

We must become free from this fear if we are to live virtuously. An example like Socrates enables us to do so. It teaches that the change which the soul undergoes at death 'will be for the better' (perhaps an echo of Socrates' words in the *Phaedo* 63) or 'at least not for the worse'.[3] This knowledge, in turn, secures one's tranquility by providing 'fearlessness towards death'.[4] Several sentences later, Plutarch explains once more the process by which such knowledge is gained:

> But the soul which endeavours, by study and the severe application of its powers of reasoning, to form an idea of what sickness, suffering, and exile really are will find much that is false and empty and corrupt in what appears to be difficulty and fearful, as the reason shows in each particular.[5]

Here, death itself is not mentioned, but the immediately prior discussion of the fear of death, coupled with Socrates' expressed willingness to die, make plain that it is the ultimate issue. The soul should re-enact via study and reason the circumstances of sickness, suffering and exile. Having worked through them, the soul can then see how hollow they are and become free from fear of them or of death.

---

1 Plutarch, *Mor.* 476A.
2 Plutarch, *Mor.* 476A.
3 Plutarch, *Mor.* 476B.
4 Plutarch, *Mor.* 476B.
5 Plutarch, *Mor.* 476D.

Obedience
Plutarch identifies that to which a philosopher should remain obedient as Nature or valiance and the quality of being high-souled. Socrates is quite ready to die rather than abandon any of this. The good man is master of his better part and must always remain true to it.

Military Context
A military context appears here in the philosopher's battle with Fortune. Socrates issues his challenge to Fortune in the passage quoted above, and it is she who makes us ill, robs us, and slanders us. Several paragraphs later, Plutarch writes that the man who has properly trained himself can say to Fortune:

> 'I have anticipated you, Fortune, and taken from you every entry whereby you might get at me', encouraged himself, not with bolts or keys or battlements, but by precepts and reasoning in which everyone who desires may share.[1]

This is yet another instance of the mythologization of the military context. Instead of fighting literal armies or tyrants (or even civil authorities), the philosopher battles a personified abstraction like Fortune.

Overcoming Physical Vulnerability
Overcoming physical vulnerability is precisely what Plutarch has in mind when he advises us to speak as Socrates did, or to form an idea of sickness, suffering, and exile. By doing so we will gain the courage and freedom to swim away from the leaky boat of the body if it appears we will crash on the shoals of vice or baseness.

Noble Deaths Connected with Sacrificial Metaphors

The above instances of the philosopher's Noble Death have not included sacrificial metaphors. This has not been a serious problem, since sacrificial metaphors were shown to be the least significant of the five components isolated in Paul and *4 Maccabees*. However, there are occurrences of the philo-

---

1 Plutarch, *Mor.* 476C.

sopher's Noble Death in which the sacrificial metaphor does appear, and these should be noted.

Tacitus on Thrasea

One such occurrence, described by Tacitus, involves the forced suicide of Thrasea, a respected senator who fell under Nero's wrath. When word of the condemnation reached Thrasea, he was deep in conversation with

> Demetrius, a master of the Cynic creed; with whom—to judge from his serious looks and the few words which caught the ear, when they chanced to raise their voices—he was debating the nature of the soul and the divorce of spirit and body.[1]

When Thrasea received the news, he asked his house-guests to leave lest they be tainted by association with a condemned man. Then he returned into his bedroom with his son-in-law and Demetrius. There, he

> offered the arteries of both arms to the knife, and, when the blood had begun to flow, sprinkled it upon the ground, and called the quaestor nearer: 'We are making a libation', and said, 'to Jove the Liberator. Look, young man, and—may Heaven, indeed, avert the omen, but you have been born into times when it is expedient to steel the mind with instances of firmness'.[2]

Vicariousness

The component of vicariousness is evident in Thrasea's admonition to the quaestor to look at the suicide and fortify himself with such an example. He should 'steel the mind' by, presumably, putting himself in Thrasea's place. In that way, he will be able to meet the demands of a dangerous time with equal nobility. The mental re-enactment of such an event was of great benefit in standing firm during a difficult period.

---

1 Tacitus, *Annals* (LCL; trans. J. Jackson; Cambridge, Mass.: Harvard University Press; London: Heinemann, 1951) 16.34.
2 Tacitus, *Annals* 16.35.

Obedience

It is not entirely clear what Thrasea is obedient to, but it does appear that he is obedient. His death is an example of firmness. What seems to be implied by the inclusion of Demetrius in the death scene is that Thrasea is dying obedient to philosophical principle, as would any good or wise man.[1] This suspicion is reinforced by the last, incomplete sentence of the *Annals*: 'Soon, as the slowness of his end brought excruciating pain, turning his gaze upon Demetrius ...'[2] It will never be known what Thrasea said, but something about the difficulty of dying in a philosophically obedient way could be expected.

Military Context

A military context is not apparent in Thrasea's death, but it is present in the events leading up to his condemnation. Marcellus, one of Nero's toadies, wonders in the Senate whether Thrasea has become a public enemy of Rome. He continues:

> A man who mourned over the nation's happiness, who treated forum and theatre and temple as a desert, who held out his own exile as a threat, must not have his perverse ambition gratified! In Thrasea's eyes, these were no senatorial resolutions; there were no magistracies, no Rome. Let him break with life, and with a country which he had long ceased to love and now to look upon![3]

Thrasea is thus depicted as an enemy of Rome, a man who in a sense is at war with the city. This depiction is, of course, at Nero's service, and is supposed to make Thrasea's condemnation look like the act of a state defending itself against hostility towards it. In reality, however, it does emphasize the extent to which men of conscience and the powers they often battle are in opposing camps.

Before leaving the topic of military context, we should note the invocation of 'Jove the Liberator'. Nero's power is not mythologized as Fortune or Fate, but the reference to libera-

---

1 In Chapter 21 of Book 16 of the *Annals*, Tacitus writes: 'After the slaughter of so many of the noble, Nero in the end conceived the ambition to extirpate virtue herself by killing Thrasea Paetus and Barea Soranus'.
2 Tacitus, *Annals* 16.35.
3 Tacitus, *Annals* 16.28.

tion by a supernatural force does recall the sort of mythologization of military context seen above.

Overcoming Physical Vulnerability

The component of overcoming physical vulnerability is clearly found in Thrasea's discussion with Demetrius on the 'divorce of spirit and body'. Thrasea must separate his mind from the excruciating pain of his death, so as to maintain obedience.

Sacrificial Metaphor

Finally, Thrasea's offering of his blood as a libation presents a sacrificial metaphor. He does not go so far as to label himself a sacrificial victim, but his statement does demonstrate that the connection between a Noble Death and the sacrificial system dedicated to the gods could be made.

Tacitus on Seneca

The same connection appears in Tacitus' account of Seneca's forced suicide. Having severed the veins in his arms and legs and consumed poison, Seneca still finds death elusive.

> In the last resort, he entered a vessel of heated water, sprinkling some on the slaves nearest, with the remark that he offered the liquid as a drink-offering to Jove the Liberator. He was then lifted into a bath, suffocated by the vapour, and cremated without ceremony.[1]

Vicariousness

That Seneca meant his death to be an example for others' benefit is a conclusion impossible to avoid. After hearing his sentence pronounced, Seneca admonishes his friends to control their grief in view of the 'maxims of philosophy' they had studied.[2] Tacitus comments that these and similar remarks could have been intended 'for a wider audience'.[3] That such a suspicion is well founded is shown by Seneca's response to his wife's request that she be allowed to commit suicide, too:

---

1 Tacitus, *Annals* 15.44.
2 Tacitus, *Annals* 15.62.
3 Tacitus, *Annals* 15.63.

> I had shown you the mitigations of life, you prefer the dis-
> tinction of death: I shall not grudge your setting that exam-
> ple. May the courage of this brave ending be divided equally
> between us both, and may more of fame attend your own
> departure![1]

Even as the blood drips from his severed veins, Seneca summons his secretaries and dictates a lengthy statement. Tacitus
does not include it since, he says, it has already been made
public.[2]

Finally, the poison that Seneca consumes when he fails to
bleed to death is hemlock—hardly a coincidence.[3]

These actions strongly indicate that this suicide is being
made a model for others to admire, draw strength from, and
emulate. Seneca's death is virtually a public event. He intends
others to have all the information they need to run through it
in their own minds and re-enact the entire sequence. By doing
this, they will gain the virtue of a philosopher and the auto-
nomy of a free man. (It should also be noted here that the
bravery of Seneca's own death must partly have come from
his long study of the Noble Deaths of others; cf. the section on
Seneca with which this chapter begins.)

Obedience

Seneca's death is, of course, a model precisely because it is in
obedience to his philosophy, to the 'maxims of philosophy' he
urges his friends to observe. Having thought about it so long,
Seneca did live up to his own best intentions, and died as a
philosopher should.

Military Context

A military context is not really present here, but Seneca is
nevertheless a victim of the same state-directed persecution
which claimed Thrasea's life.

Overcoming Physical Vulnerability

The theme of overcoming physical vulnerability is presupposed throughout. Seneca does not in any way let Nero's

1 Tacitus, *Annals* 15.43.
2 Tacitus, *Annals* 15.63.
3 Tacitus, *Annals* 15.64.

power over his physical being frighten or intimidate him. Even the agonizing slowness of his end does not deter Seneca from his inner purpose.

Sacrificial Metaphor
The sacrificial metaphor here is not precisely the same as in the story about Thrasea. That is, Seneca does not sprinkle drops of his blood and call them a libation. Rather, he sprinkles drops of water. He is in the water at the time, however, and so the connection with himself and his death seems clear. Once again, a philosopher's death is characterized by a sacrificial metaphor. The dedication to Jove the Liberator is, of course, the same as with Thrasea.

Lucian on Demonax
Lucian provides a good example of a philosopher's death metaphorized as a sacrifice in his tribute to Demonax. When he, like Socrates, was hauled before the Athenian assembly on charges of impiety, he began his address thus:

> Men of Athens, you see me ready with my garland: come, sacrifice (*katathuein*) me like your former victim, for on that occasion your offering found no favour with the gods![1]

Vicariousness
Demonax is clearly re-enacting Socrates' death. He tells the Athenians he is ready for them to sacrifice him just as they did Socrates. Presumably, the knowledge of how glorious Socrates' death really was helps Demonax to take this firm stand, as it must have fortified him every time he mentally ran through it in his philosophical training. Demonax's own death is not specifically labeled as a model for others, but his willingness to die for philosophy is doubtless included in what Lucian finds so admirable when he says:

> It is now fitting to tell of Demonax for two reasons—that he may be retained in memory by men of culture as far as I can bring it about, and that young men of good instincts who

---

1 Lucian, 'Demonax', *The Works of Lucian* (LCL; trans. A.M. Harmon; Cambridge, Mass.: Harvard University Press; London: Heinemann, 1961) vol. 1, section 11.

aspire to philosophy may not have to shape themselves by
ancient precedents (*paradeigmata*) alone, but may be able to
set themselves a pattern from our modern world and to copy
that man, the best of all the philosophers whom I know
about.[1]

Here is seen the now familiar idea of copying a pattern.
Lucian offers Demonax—along with his willingness to die—as
a pattern for the young to assimilate in their own lives.

Obedience

The question of obedience is involved in Demonax's legal self-
defense, for he makes plain that he will not abandon his philosophical principles: he has not sacrificed to Athena because 'I
did not suppose that she had need of my offerings'; he has not
joined the Eleusinian Mysteries because, if they were evil, he
would warn others away, while if they were good, he would
explain them to everyone 'out of his love for humanity'.[2] Even
though sacrifices to Athena and the Mysteries are an important, seemingly harmless part of civic life, Demonax will not
participate in them. He fears that doing so would violate his
philosophical precepts of truth and virtue. If the Athenians
want to execute him for his obedience, he is prepared to emulate his master and drink poison.

Military Context

There is no explicit military context to Lucian's essay on
Demonax, beyond the latter's determination to battle for what
he believes and his willingness to engage an entire *polis* in
conflict.

Overcoming Physical Vulnerability

Demonax has obviously overcome any anxiety regarding his
physical vulnerability. He stands ready to be executed, if need
be. No doubt he would hold up nicely under torture, too. The
extent to which he had overcome concerns about his bodily
welfare is shown by the following:

1 Lucian, 'Demonax' section 2.
2 Lucian, 'Demonax' section 11.

A short time before the end he was asked: 'What orders have you to give about your burial?' and replied: 'Don't borrow trouble! The stench will get me buried'! The man said: 'Why, isn't it disgraceful that the body of such a man should be exposed for birds and dogs to devour?' 'I see nothing out of the way in it', said he, 'if even in death I am going to be a service to living things'.[1]

Sacrificial Metaphor

Demonax describes both himself and Socrates as sacrifices. He appears before the Athenians garlanded like a sacrificial animal.

Summary of Philosophers' Sacrificial Deaths

This brief survey of philosophers' sacrificial deaths shows that, while the Noble Death was not consistently linked with sacrifice, the conceptual basis for such a connection existed and the latter was occasionally made.

Summary

This chapter has demonstrated the occurrence of the first four components of the Noble Death in Seneca, Epictetus, Silius Italicus, and Plutarch. It has then proceeded to document the sacrificial component of the Noble Death in Tacitus and Lucian. The result is that the Noble Death has been exhibited as known and utilized by a broad spectrum of Greco-Roman writers around the time of the New Testament. Its integrity and familiarity during this period are well attested.

---

1 Lucian, 'Demonax' section 66.

CONCLUSION

Jesus' death in Paul is vicarious. That is, it has an effect which reaches beyond Jesus himself and provides benefit to others. This proposition is hardly debatable, for it is supported by any number of statements within the Pauline corpus (e.g. Rom. 3.24-26; 4.25; 8.32; 1 Cor. 15.3; Gal. 2.20; 3.13). What is debatable is the issue of precisely how Jesus' death is vicarious. Which interpretive construct has Paul used to express the vicariousness of Jesus' death? Is the latter vicarious after the fashion of a cultic sacrifice? Does Paul employ the figure of the Suffering Servant or that of Isaac in Genesis 22 as models? Has he understood Jesus' death along the line of a Mystery deity? Or does he conceive of Jesus as a martyr? These, it seems, are the major options offered by New Testament scholarship for understanding just how Paul formulates Jesus' vicarious death.

We have sorted through each of these options, determined their relative value, and then provided our own answer based on the conception of martyrdom. Chapter 1 examined traces of the Temple cultus in Paul's interpretation of Jesus' death, but concluded that they did not have a formative impact on Paul's thought. The same conclusion was reached in Chapter 2 regarding the Suffering Servant, and in Chapter 3 with respect to the Binding of Isaac.

As the reader saw, careful exegesis often rendered doubtful the assertion that a given pericope alludes to the cultus, the Servant, or the Akedah. However, even when such allusions are sustained, the telling point is that Paul does not develop them for his own soteriological purposes. Time after time it was found that he leaves them in isolated, usually traditional units and instead uses what has been called 'aeon-categories'. These refer to spheres of power which Paul depicts as ruled by either Jesus or Sin. These spheres divide human existence between them. A person's life is run by one or the other. Jesus' death is the point where a transference occurs that shifts the believer from the sphere of Sin into Jesus' sphere. Chapters 1–3 did not attempt to explicate just how these aeon-categories operate in Paul's soteriology. They simply pointed out these categories' importance. The task of determining how they fit into Paul's understanding of Jesus' vicarious death was left to Chapter 5.

Chapter 4 did not proceed, as had Chapters 1–3, through detailed exegesis. This is because its subject was the Mysteries. We know that Paul could have had relatively easy access to the data of the cultus, the Suffering Servant, and the Akedah. He had only to visit the Temple or open the Hebrew Scriptures. Therefore, commentators need merely point to catchwords or Scriptural citations which presumably refer to these data. (It is this presumptive ease of reference which necessitated the close exegesis of Chapters 1–3 in the first place.) But we do not know that Paul had the same sort of access to the Mysteries. Nor does he employ terminology from them.[1] Hence, it is crucial for the 'Mystery thesis' to establish the currency of ideas about the vicarious deaths of Mystery deities. The job of determining whether such ideas were in fact abroad must involve an analysis of the Mysteries themselves.

Chosen for this analysis were the four Mystery deities Adonis, Attis, Osiris and Isis, along with the Eleusinian cult. The first three were picked because of their traditional prominence in this regard,[2] the fourth because of her widespread popularity during the period,[3] and the last because of its antiquity and notoriety at this time. As far as possible, primary texts were consulted and the question was asked whether worshippers participated somehow in a vicarious death of the tutelary deity. The answer with respect to all five items examined was either 'no' or 'doubtful'. Attestations for the very death of Adonis are surprisingly scarce. Those sources which do describe his passage between Earth and the Under-

1 A.D. Nock, 'Hellenistic Mysteries and Christian Sacraments', *Essays on Religion and the Ancient World* (2 vols; ed. Z. Stewart; Cambridge, Mass.: Harvard University Press, 1972) 2.809.

2 J.G. Frazer, *Adonis, Attis, Osiris* (New York: Macmillan, 1906).

3 Cf. *inter alia*, F. Dunand, *Le culte d'Isis dans le bassin oriental de la Méditerrannée* (EPRO, 26; 3 vols; Leiden: Brill, 1973); R.E. Witt, *Isis in the Greco-Roman World* (Ithaca, New York: Cornell University Press, 1971).

world seem to regard it more as simple movement than as a cycle of death/rebirth. Evidence for the death of Attis is even more difficult to gain. Apuleius' remarks about Osiris in the *Metamorphoses* are suggestive, but the descriptions of the actual rituals are either too brief for reasonable speculation or absent altogether. As for Isis, she did not die. The Eleusinian cult's references to the descent of Persephone and Demeter into the Underworld seem, as with Adonis, more directed towards a journey than a death.

Chapter 5 took up the question of martyrs and began to develop a new solution to the problem of the background of Pauline soteriology. It started with an examination of E. Lohse's thesis that early Christian interpretations of Jesus' death are indebted to Palestinian Jewish concepts regarding the deaths of martyrs. It was found that Lohse's own evidence belies the orientation of his theory. His analyses of martyrs' deaths in 2 and 4 Maccabees are provocative and promising, but both texts evince a Hellenistic provenance, and cannot be locked into a Palestinian setting as Lohse wants to do. (He uses a sharp distinction between Hellenistic and Palestinian which is, in any case, outmoded.)[1] K. Wengst and S.K. Williams have seen this difficulty and, in their treatments of 2 and 4 Maccabees, have simply abandoned Lohse's efforts to keep them free from Hellenistic influence. Their lead was followed, with results that became most evident in Chapter 6.

Chapter 5 also found that 2 Maccabees does not contain examples of vicarious, expiatory death (as is sometimes maintained). That is to say, there are not deaths which benefit other people through working out or somehow canceling their sins. But there is one death (Eleazar's) which benefits others mimetically. The word 'mimetically' is used here to indicate that Eleazar's death provides others with a model or pattern for correct behavior. People can become inspired by his example, and by putting themselves in the old man's place, they re-enact his death in their own imaginations. In mentally bearing up under the tortures he went through, they come to see that they, too, can win victory by endurance should they have

---

1 Hengel, *Judaism and Hellenism*; Smith, *Palestinian Parties* ch. 3.

to do so literally. An imaginative imitation prepares and strengthens them for the real thing.

The people who benefit from Eleazer's death fall into two groups. The first consists of the youths among Eleazer's fellow-citizens (6.24; 28). The second consists of the audience reading *2 Maccabees* (cf. especially 6.20). Both groups become aware of the martyrs through story. This is obviously the case with readers of *2 Maccabees*. It is presumably so with the youths as well, since they seem not to have been present at the executions, and would have had to hear (or read) about them later. More will be said about this below.

Analysis of *2 Maccabees* also showed three more elements (beyond vicariousness) of particular importance with regard to Eleazer's death. The first is obedience. This, of course, is what makes Eleazer a martyr. If he had failed to maintain obedience to the Law, his death would not have been admirable or worth imitating. The second element is a military context. Eleazer is caught up in a war between Antiochus, his army, and the Hellenizers on the one hand, and those who follow the Law on the other. The third is overcoming physical vulnerability. It is the latter which Antiochus Epiphanes plays upon in order to get the old man to disobey. His efforts are in vain, however, for Eleazer's devotion to the Law overcomes the pain inflicted on his body. These four elements (vicariousness, obedience, military context, and overcoming physical vulnerability), plus a fifth, less important one (sacrificial metaphor) were termed the Noble Death.

The utility and substantive character of this cluster was demonstrated via its discovery in *4 Maccabees* as well. The deaths of the martyrs in *4 Maccabees* are indeed vicarious, a fact about which there has never been any serious debate. But the mode of their vicariousness was shown to be fundamentally mimetic, as with *2 Maccabees*. The sacrificial language which appears at 6.29 and 17.21-22 is marked as figural, while the real means by which the martyrs' deaths benefit others is through imitation. By inspiring their fellow citizens to follow their example, the martyrs make it impossible for Antiochus to enforce his decrees, whereupon he leaves (18.5).

In addition, the author of *4 Maccabees* explicitly uses the martyrs as examples to be followed by his own audience. Here the vicariousness of their deaths operates mimetically in terms of story. By mentally tracing each grisly detail (which the author makes sure they do), the listeners/readers imaginatively re-enact the martyrs' deaths. This strengthens them in case it should be necessary to re-enact the deaths literally (cf. 7.8-9; 14.9).

Hence, the role of story or narrative seems critical in conveying the vicarious effect of the martyrs' deaths in *4 Maccabees*. The author's audience is invited into the story, as just indicated. And, since it would have been impossible for very many people actually to witness the deaths, the vicarious effect on the martyrs' fellow-citizens presumably functioned through story as well.

The other four elements of the Noble Death (obedience, military context, overcoming physical vulnerability, and sacrificial metaphors) are readily discernable in *4 Maccabees*. Obedience comes in for special stress in *4 Maccabees*. By dying obediently, the martyrs are able to claim victory over Antiochus. They render futile his efforts to compel them to abandon the Law (9.30; 11.24-25; cf. also 1.11).

All of the elements just noted are located in Paul in the final segment of Chapter 5.

That Jesus' death is vicarious in Paul needs little argument, as stated above. But the mode of this vicariousness does bear investigation. It turns out to be mimetic. In the same way that the beneficiaries of the vicarious effect of the martyrs' deaths imaginatively re-enact those deaths through hearing or reading the story, the beneficiaries of the vicarious effect of Jesus' death re-enact his death through a ritualized version of the story. In Romans 6, Paul asserts that believers die with Christ during baptism, i.e. they re-enact his death in their own lives. Paul is very eager to make sure that the Romans understand how baptism fits into the story of Jesus' death. That is why he says in 6.3 'Do you not know that all of us who have been baptised into Christ Jesus were baptised into his death?' By re-enacting Jesus' death in this way, they are transferred from the aeon of Sin to the aeon ruled by him.

In putting things thus, Paul has coalesced the two categories of literal and imaginative re-enactment. The beneficiary of the vicarious effect of a martyrs' death imaginatively re-enacts that death, being strengthened thereby in case a literal re-enactment becomes necessary. Paul has rendered the process of re-enacting Christ's death so that, when the believer 'reads' his or her own life in terms of Christ's story, this is not merely an imaginative re-enactment, but one with the sort of objective effect that pertains to the literal re-enactment of a martyrs' death. When one copies a martyrs' death and dies obediently, one gains a victory over the evil tyrant whose compulsions have proved ineffective. When one 'dies with' Christ, even though one does not literally die, one gains liberation from and shares in a victory over the evil tyrant Sin. Paul seems to think that the act of 'dying with' Christ ritually creates virtually the same sort of disjunction customarily associated with literal death. One is no longer ruled by Sin because one is no longer that person, exactly. Although Paul seems also to have believed that some sort of personal continuity remained between the individual who died with Christ and the individual who emerged, he nevertheless emphasized the fissure between old and new very strongly. Precisely how he conceived all this is not spelled out in his letters. Perhaps such a strange and perplexing event could not be fully explicated. It is clear, however, that for Paul a re-enactment (in ritual) of Christ's death by the believer was critical.

The presence of the remaining four elements of the Noble Death (obedience, military context, overcoming physical vulnerability, and sacrificial metaphors) leaves little doubt that Paul is, indeed, utilizing it. Rom. 5.18-19 and Phil. 2.7 show that Jesus' death is obedient. Paul's use of combat metaphors to express the battle between the aeons demonstrates a military context. As for overcoming physical vulnerability, this element can be perceived in Jesus' career if one considers the implications of the anthropology in Romans 7 for Pauline Christology. In Romans 7, Paul indicates that sin works through the flesh (i.e. physical vulnerability) to contradict the inner man's righteous inclination. But assertions about Jesus' obedience (see above) and sinlessness (cf. 2 Cor. 5.21) show that Jesus must somehow have overcome the physical vulnerability of the human condition and resisted Sin's compulsion.

Finally, there is definitely sacrificial language in Paul, although Chapter 2 has shown it to be ancillary (as it is in *4 Maccabees*).

In Chapter 6, the literature of Greco-Roman popular philosophy was taken up. This was for two reasons: (1) the strongly Hellenistic features of *2* and *4 Maccabees*, (2) the failed promise of Old Testament options like the cultus, the Suffering Servant, and the Akedah. The wisdom of this move quickly became clear. Analysis of Seneca, Epictetus, Silius Italicus, and others demonstrated that the Noble Death was at home in the Greco-Roman world and had become a virtual commonplace by the first century CE. Examples of philosophical martyrs were consciously collected and followed. Indeed, Seneca indicates that each moment of life should be patterned after them.

By imaginatively re-enacting the Noble Deaths of figures like Socrates or Cato, one gains freedom from the fear and compulsion of death or fate. Indeed, the extent to which these abstractions are personified puts the Noble Death of the philosopher-martyr closer to Jesus' death in Paul (with its use of aeon-categories like Sin) than were the deaths of the Maccabeean martyrs. Socrates is said to have freed mankind from the fear of death, Scipio to have defeated death, and Cato to have frustrated the efforts of Fortune against him. It is also said of Cato that Nature brought her power against him so that everyone would know the catastrophes which followed were not real ills.

If an author like Seneca had had an even stronger sense of the victory one gains over death, Fortune, or Nature through the imaginative re-enactment of the philosopher-martyr's death, he might have regarded it as the first fruits of immortality. Had such been the case, he would have then presented an almost exact replica of the pattern in Paul. (There would still remain the difference that, in Paul, Jesus is the *only* one who could ever personally triumph over the mythic foe by dying obediently; everyone else is overwhelmed by the compelling force of Sin working through fleshly, physical vulnerability.)

The other four elements of the Noble Death (obedience, military context, overcoming physical vulnerability, and sacrificial metaphors) are not hard to find in Greco-Roman philosophical literature. Seneca is anxious to have the philosopher remain obedient to his philosophy. Epictetus is concerned that the philosopher fulfill his mission obediently. A military context is provided by the fact that most figures held up as examples are either literal soldiers or figurative ones in battles against Fortune, Nature, etc. Overcoming physical vulnerability is a pervasive consideration; like the author of *4 Maccabees*, these writers are very concerned with enduring torture. And, as just noted, the hardships of which they speak are often inflicted by a mythic enemy, placing them in line with Paul. Finally, Chapter 6 showed that the Noble Death of the philosopher-martyr could and did have sacrificial metaphors applied to it. Seneca's own death is so described by Tacitus.

What this study has shown is that Paul was very much a man of his time. When he interpreted Jesus' death, he did not use the Temple cultus (a phenomenon which had nothing to do with *human* sacrifice). Neither did he use Hebrew Bible passages with no history of suitable interpretation (i.e. Isa. 52–53 or Gen. 22). Nor did he employ the Mysteries. Instead, he used a notion available to anyone who breathed the intellectual atmosphere of the Hellenistic Kingdoms and the early Roman Empire. This was the Noble Death. It seems to have come to Paul quite naturally and to have been at hand for him to employ after his own fashion. That he knew he was doing so is questionable. He may not have thought of interpreting Jesus' death otherwise. Nonetheless, this does not efface the Noble Death's presence or lessen its importance in his work.

BIBLIOGRAPHY

Aalen, S., 'Das Abendmahl als Opfermahl im Neuen Testament', *NovT* 6 (1963), pp. 128-52.

Allo, E.-B., *Première Épître aux Corinthiens* (2nd edn, Paris: Librairie Lecoffre, 1956).

Althaus, P., *Der Brief an die Römer* (NTO, 6; 9th edn, Göttingen: Vandenhoeck & Ruprecht, 1959).

Appollodorus, *The Library* (LCL; translated by J.G. Frazer; London: Heinemann; New York: Putnam, 1921).

Apuleius, *The Golden Ass*, translated by W. Adlington; revised by S. Gaselee (LCL; London: Heinemann; New York: Putnam, 1919).

—*The Isis-Book*, edited by J.G. Griffiths (ERRO, 39; Leiden: Brill, 1975).

Aristophanes, *Aristophanes*, translated by B.B. Rogers (LCL; London: Heinemann; New York: Putnam, 1924).

Athenaeus, *The Deipnosophists*, translated by C.B. Gulick (LCL; London: Heinemann; New York: Putnam, 1927-41).

Bachmann, P., *Der erste Brief des Paulus an die Korinther* (4th edn, Leipzig: Deichertsche Verlagsbuchhandlung, 1936).

Barrett, C.K., *A Commentary on the Epistle to the Romans* (New York: Harper, 1957).

Bartchy, S. Scott, 'Table Fellowship with Jesus and the "Lord's Meal" at Corinth', *Increase in Learning: Essays in Honor of James G. Van Buren*, edited by R.O. Owens, Jr & B.E. Hamm (Manhatten, Kansas: Manhatten Christian College, 1979), pp. 45-61.

Barth, M., *Das Abendmahl* (ThS, 18; Zürich: Zollikon, 1945).

Bauer, W., *Das Johannesevangelium*, 2nd edn (HNT, 6; Tübingen: Mohr [Paul Siebeck], 1925).

Beare, F.W., *A Commentary on the Epistle to the Philippians* (HNTC; New York: Harper, 1959).

Behm, J., 'ἔσω', *TDNT* 2 (1964), pp. 698-99.

—'θύω', *TDNT* 3 (1965), pp. 180-90.

Beker, J.C., *Paul the Apostle* (Philadelphia: Fortress, 1980).

Betz, H.D., *Galatians: A Commentary on Paul's Letter to the Churches in Galatia* (Hermeneia; Philadelphia: Fortress, 1979).

Betz, J., *Die Realpräsenz des Leibes und Blutes Jesu im Abendmahl nach dem Neuen Testament*; Vol. 2, Part 1 of *Die Eucharistie in der Zeit der Griechischen Väter* (Freiburg, Basel & Vienna: Herder, 1961).

Bevan, E.R., 'Mystery Religions', *The History of Christianity in the Light of Modern Knowledge* (New York: Harcourt, Brace, 1929).

Beyer, H.-W., and Althaus, P., *Der Brief an die Galater* (NTD, 8; 10th edn; Göttingen: Vandenhoeck & Ruprecht, 1965).

Bickermann, E., 'The Date of Fourth Maccabees' *Louis Ginzberg Jubilee Volume* (New York: The American Academy for Jewish Research, 1945), pp. 105-12.

Blank, J., 'Der gespaltene Mensch, Zur Exegese von Röm. 7.7-25', *Bibel und Leben* 9 (1968), pp. 10-20.

—*Paulus und Jesus* (StANT, 18; Munich: Kösel, 1968).

Blass, F., Debrunner, A., and Rehkopf, F., *Grammatik des neutestamentlichen Griechisch* 14th edn (Göttingen: Vandenhoeck & Ruprecht, 1976).

Boers, H.W., 'Apocalyptic Eschatology in I Corinthians 15', *Int* 21 (1967), pp. 50-65.

Bonhöffer, A., *Epiktet und das Neue Testament* (RVV, 10; Giessen: Töpelmann, 1911).

Bornkamm, G., 'Lord's Supper and Church in Paul', *Early Christian Experience*, translated by P.L. Hammer (New York & Evanston, Illinois: Harper & Row, 1969), pp. 123-60.

—'On Understanding the Christ-Hymn', *Early Christian Experience* (New York & Evanston, Illinois: Harper & Row, 1969), pp. 112-22.

Bousset, W., 'Der erste Brief an die Korinther', *Die Schriften des Neuen Testaments*, 2nd edn, edited by J. Weiss (Göttingen: Vandenhoeck & Ruprecht, 1908).

Brandenburger, E., *Adam und Christus* (WMANT, 7; Neukirchen-Vluyn: Neukirchener Verlag, 1962).

—*Fleisch und Geist* (WMANT, 29; Neukirchen-Vluyn: Neukirchener Verlag, 1968).

Braun, H., 'Römer 7.7-25 und das Selbstverständnis des Qumran-Frommen', *ZTK* 56 (1959), pp. 1-18.

Breitenstein, U., *Beobachtungen zu Sprache, Stil und Gendankengut des Vierten Makkabäerbuchs*, 2nd edn (Basel: Schwabe, 1978).

Brinsmead, B.H., *Galatians–Dialogical Response to Opponents* (SBLDS, 65; Chico, California: Scholars Press, 1982).

Brox, N., *Zeuge und Märtyrer* (StANT, 5; Munich: Kösel, 1961).

Bruce, F.F., *The Epistle to the Galatians* (NIGTC; Grand Rapids: Eerdmans, 1982).

—*The Epistle of Paul to the Romans* (Grand Rapids: Eerdmans, 1963).

—*1 and 2 Corinthians* (London: Marshall, Morgan & Scott, 1971).

Brunner, E., *Der Römerbrief* (Kassel: Oncken, 1938).

Bultmann, R., 'Neueste Paulusforschung' *TR* 8 (1936), pp. 11-12.

—'The Problem of Ethics in the Writings of Paul', *The Old and New Man* (Richmond, Virginia: John Knox, 1967), pp. 7-32.

—*Theology of the New Testament*, 2 volumes, translated by K. Grobel (New York: Scribner, 1951).

Burkert, W., *Greek Religion* translated by J. Raffan (Cambridge, Massachusetts: Harvard University Press, 1985).

—*Structure and History in Greek Mythology and Ritual* (SCS, 47; Berkeley: University of California Press, 1979).

Bussmann, C., 'Christus starb für unsere Sünden', *Biblische Randbemerkungen*, 2nd edn, edited by H. Merklein & J. Lange (Würzburg: Echter-Verlag, 1974), pp. 337-45.

Caird, G.B., *Principalities and Powers* (Oxford: Clarendon, 1956).

Cangh, J.M. van., '"Mort pour nos péchés selon les Écritures" (1 Co 15.3b) Une référence à Isaïe 53?', *Revue Théologique du Louvain* 1/2 (1970), pp. 191-99.

Carpenter, L.L., *Primitive Christian Application of the Doctrine of the Servant* (Durham, North Carolina: Duke University Press, 1929).

Cerfaux, L., *Christ in the Theology of St. Paul*, translated by G. Webb & A. Walker (Freiburg, Basel & Vienna: Herder, 1959).

Charles, R.H., ed. *The Apocrypha and Pseudepigrapha of the Old Testament*, 2 vols. (Oxford: Oxford University Press, 1913).

Clement of Alexandria, 'The Exhortation to the Greeks', *Clement of Alexandria*, translated by G.W. Butterworth (London: Heinemann; New York: Putnam, 1919).

Cole, S.G., 'New Evidence for the Mysteries of Dionysos', *GRBS* 21 (1980), pp. 223-38.

Collins, J.J., 'Testaments', *Jewish Writings of the Second Temple Period*, compendia Rerum Iudaicarum ad Novum Testamentum, Section Two, Vol. 2, edited by M. Stone, (Assen: Van Gorcum; Philadelphia: Fortress, 1984), pp. 325-55.

Colpe, C., 'Zur mythologischen Struktur der Adonis-, Attis- und Osiris-Überlieferungen', *lišan mithurti* (AOAT, 1; in cooperation with M. Dietrich, edited by W. Rollig; Kevelaer: Butzon & Bercker; Neukirchen-Vluyn: Neukirchener Verlag, 1969), pp. 23-44.

Conzelmann, H., *1 Corinthians: A Commentary on the First Epistle to the Corinthians*, translated by J.W. Leitch, bibliography and references by J.W. Dunkly, edited by G.W. MacRae (Philadelphia: Fortress, 1975).

—'On the Analysis of the Confessional Formula in 1 Corinthians 15.3-5', *Int* 20 (1966), pp. 15-25.

—*An Outline of the Theology of the New Testament* (New York and Evanston, Illinois: Harper, 1969).

Corriveau, R., *The Liturgy of Life* (Studia, Travaux de recherche, 25; Brussels and Paris: Brouwer; Montreal: Bellarmin, 1970).

Cousar, C.B., *Galatians* (Atlanta: John Knox Press, 1982).

Cranfield, C.E.B., *A Critical and Exegetical Commentary on The Epistle to the Romans*, 2 volumes (ICC, 82; Edinburgh: Clark, 1975-77).

Cullmann, O., ' "KYRIOS" as Designation for the Oral Tradition concerning Jesus' *SJT* 3 (1950), pp. 180-97.

Dahl, N., 'The Atonement—An Adequate Reward for the Akedah? (Rom. 8.32)', *Neotestamentica et Semitica*, edited by E.E. Ellis and M. Wilcox (Edinburgh: Clark, 1969), pp. 15-29.

Daly, R., *Christian Sacrifice* (SCA, 18; Washington, D.C.: The Catholic University of America Press, 1978).

Davies, P.R., 'Passover and the Dating of the Aqedah', *JSS* 30, (1979), pp. 59-67.

Davies, W.D., *Paul and Rabbinic Judaism*, 4th edn (Philadelphia: Fortress, 1980).

Deichgräber, R., *Gotteshymnus und Christushymnus in der frühen Christenheit* (SUNT, 5; Göttingen: Vandenhoeck & Ruprecht, 1967).

Delling, G., *Der Kreuzestod Jesu in der urchristlichen Verkündigung* (Göttingen: Vandenhoeck & Ruprecht, 1972).

—'The Significance of the Resurrection of Jesus for Faith in Jesus Christ', *The Significance of the Message of the Resurrection for Faith in Jesus Christ*, translated by D.M. Barton & R.A. Wilson, edited by C.F.D. Moule (SBT, 8; second series; Naperville, Illinois: Allenson, 1968), pp. 77-104.

Dibelius, M., 'The Isis Initiation in Apuleius and Related Initiatory Rites', *Conflict at Colossae*, edited and translated by F.O. Francis and W.A. Meeks (Sources for Biblical Study, 4; revised edn, Missoula, Montana: Society of Biblical Literature & Scholars Press, 1975), pp. 61-122.

Dinkler, E., 'Die Verkündigung als eschatologisch-sakramentales Geschehen. Auslegung von 2 Kor 5.14-16.2', *Die Zeit Jesu*, edited by G. Bornkamm and K. Rahner (Freiburg, Basel & Vienna: Herder, 1970), pp. 169-89.

Dodd, C.H., *According to the Scriptures* (Digswell Place, Great Britain: Nisbet, 1961).

—*The Epistle of Paul to the Romans* (Moffatt New Testament Commentary, 6; New York: Harper, 1932).

Döring, K., *Exemplum Socratis* (Hermes, Zeitschrift für klassische Philologie, Einzelschriften, 42; Wiesbaden: Steiner, 1979).

Duchrow, U., *Christenheit und Weltantwortung* (FBESAWK, 25; Stuttgart: Klett, 1970).

Dunand, F., *Le culte d'Isis dans le bassin oriental de la Mediterrannée*, 3 volumes (EPRO, 26; Leiden: Brill, 1973).

Dunn, J.D.G., *Christology in the Making* (Philadelphia: Westminster, 1980).

Duthoy, R., *The Tauroboleum: Its Evolution and Terminology* (Leiden: Brill, 1969).

Eichholz, G., *Die Theologie des Paulus im Umriss* (Neukirchen-Vluyn: Neukirchener Verlag, 1972).

Eissfeldt, O., *The Old Testament*, translated by P.R. Ackroyd (New York & Evanston, Illinois: Harper & Row, 1965).

Epictetus, 'Discourses', *The Discourses as Reported by Arrian, The Manual, and Fragments*, translated by W.A. Oldfather (LCL; Cambridge, Massachusetts: Harvard University Press; London: Heinemann, 1966).

Ernst, J., *Die Briefe an die Philipper, an Philemon, an die Klosser, an die Epheser* (RNS, 7; Part 3; Regensburg: Pustet, 1974).

Euler, K.F., *Die Verkündigung vom leidenden Gottesknecht aus Jes 53 in der griechischen Bibel* (Stuttgart & Berlin: Kohlhammer, 1934).

Fascher, E., *Jesaja 53 in christlicher und jüdischer Sicht* (AVTRW, 4; Berlin: Evangelische Verlagsanstalt, n.d.).

Ferguson, W.S., 'The Attic Orgeones' *HTR*, 37; (1944), pp. 61-130.

Feuillet, A., 'L'hymme christologique de l'épître aux Philippiens (II.6-11)', *RB* 72 (1965), pp. 481-507.

Firmicus Maternus, *Firmicus Maternus: The Error of the Pagan Religions*, translated by C.A. Forbes (ACW, 37; New York & Ramsey, New Jersey: Norman, 1970).

Fitzer, G., 'Der Ort der Versöhnung nach Paulus', *TZ* 22 (1966), pp. 161-83.

Fitzmyer, J., 'The Languages of First Century Palestine', *CBQ* 32 (1970), pp. 501-31.

—Review of A.D. Macho, *Neophyti 1*, *CBQ* 32 (1970), pp. 106-13.

—Review of M. McNamara, *The New Testament and the Palestinian Targum to the Pentateuch*, *TS* 29 (1968), pp. 322-26.

—*Ancient Egyptian Religion* (New York: Columbia University Press, 1948).

Frankfort, H., *Kingship and the Gods* (Chicago: The University of Chicago Press, 1948).

Frazer, J.G., *Adonis, Attis, Osiris* (New York: Macmillan, 1906).

Friedrich, G., 'Der Brief an die Philipper,' *Die kleineren Briefe des Apostels Paulus* (editors: H.W. Beyer, P.Althaus, H.Conzelmann, G. Friedrich, A. Oepke; 9th edn; NTD, 8; Göttingen: Vandenhoeck & Ruprecht, 1962), pp. 92-129.

—'Das Gesetz des Glaubens Röm. 3.27', *TZ* 10 (1954), pp. 401-17.

—*Die Verkündigung des Todes Jesu im Neuen Testament* (BTS, 6; Neukirchen-Vluyn: Neukirchener Verlag, 1982).

Füglister, N., *Die Heilsbedeutung des Pascha* (StANT, 8: Munich: Kösel, 1963).

Furness, J.M. 'Behind the Philippian Hymn', *ExpT* 79 (1968), pp. 178-81.

Furnish, V.P., *Theology and Ethics in Paul* (Nashville: Abingdon, 1968).

Gaugler, E., *Der Römerbrief*, 2 volumes (SBG; Zürich: Zwingli, 1958).

Georgi, D., 'Der vorpaulinische Hymnus Phil 2.6-11', *Zeit und Geschichte*, edited by E. Dinkler (Tübingen: Mohr [Paul Siebeck], 1964), pp. 263-93.

Gese, H., *Zur biblischen Theologie* (Munich: Christian Kaiser Verlag, 1977).

Gifford, E.H., *The Epistle of St. Paul to the Romans* (London: Murray, 1886).

Gnilka, J., *Der Philipperbrief*, Fascicle 3, (HThK, 10; Freiburg, Basel & Vienna: Herder, 1968).

Godet, F., *Commentary on St. Paul's Epistle to the Romans*, translated by A. Cusin, edited by T.W. Chambers, 2nd edn of translation (New York: Funk & Wagnalls, 1883).

Goldstein, J.A., *II Maccabees* (AB, 1a; Garden City, N.Y.: Doubleday, 1983).

Gow, A.S.F., 'The *Adoniazusae* of Theocritus', *JHS* 58 (1938), pp. 180-204.

Graillo, H., *Le culte de Cybèle, mère des dieux, à Rome et dans l'Empire romain* (Bibliotheque des Écoles françaises d'Anthènes et de Rome, 107; Paris: Fontemoing, 1912).

Greenfield, J.C., Review of J.W. Etheridge, *The Targums of Onkelos and Jonathan ben Uzziel on the Pentateuch, with the Fragments of the Jerusalem Targum from the Chaldee*, *JBL* 89 (1970), pp. 238-39.

Gressmann, H., *Die orientalischen Religionen im hellenistisch-römischen Zeitalter* (Berlin and Leipzig: de Gruyter, 1930).

—'Ἡ κοινωνία τῶν δαιμονίων', *ZNW* 20 (1921), pp. 224-30.

Gubler, M.-L., *Die frühesten Deutungen des Todes Jesu* (OBO, 15; Schweiz: Universitätsverlag Freiburg; Göttingen: Vandenhoeck & Ruprecht, 1977).

Guthrie, D., *Galatians*, The Century Bible, New Series (London: Nelson, 1969).

Hadas, M., *The Third and Fourth Books of Maccabees* (New York: Harper, 1953).

Hahn, F., *The Titles of Jesus in Christology* (LL; New York & Cleveland: The World Publishing Co., 1969).

Hays, R.B., *The Faith of Jesus Christ* (SBLDS, 56; Chico, California: Scholars Press, 1983).

Hayward, R., 'The Present State of Research into the Targumic Account of the Sacrifice of Isaac', *JJS* 32 (1981), pp. 127-50.

Hengel, M., *Judaism and Hellenism*, 2 volumes, translated by J. Bowden (Philadelphia: Fortress, 1973).

Hepding, H., *Attis, seine Mythen und sein Kult* (RVV, 1; Giessen: Töpelmann, 1903).

Higgins, A.J.B., *The Lord's Supper in the New Testament* (SBT, 6; London: SCM, 1956).

Hill, D., *Greek Words and Hebrew Meanings: Studies in the Semantics of Soteriological Terms* (SNTSMS, 5; Cambridge: Cambridge University Press, 1967).

Hillyer, N., 'The Servant of God', *EvQ* 41 (1969), pp. 143-60.

Hofius, O., *Der Christushymnus Philipper 2.6-11* (WUNT, 17; Tübingen: Mohr (Paul Siebeck), 1976).

Hommel, H., 'Das 7. Kapitel des Römerbriefs im Licht antiker Überlieferung', *Theologia Viatorum*, volume 8, edited by F. Mass (Berlin: De Gruyter, 1962), pp. 90-116.

Hooker, M.D., *Jesus and the Servant* (London: SPCK, 1959).

—'Phil. 2.6-11', *Jesus und Paulus*, edited by E.E. Ellis and E. Grässer (Göttingen: Vandenhoeck & Ruprecht, 1975), pp. 151-64.

Jeremias, J., 'Artikelloses χριστός. Zur Ursprache von 1 Cor 15.3b-5', *ZNW* 57 (1966), pp. 211-15.

—*Die Abendmahlsworte Jesu*, 4th edn (Göttingen: Vandenhoeck & Ruprecht, 1967).

—*The Eucharistic Words of Jesus*, translated by N. Perrin (New York: Scribner, 1966).

—*Der Opfertod Jesu Christ* (Calwer Hefte, 62; 2nd edn; Stuttgart: Calwer, 1966).

—'πάσχα', *TDNT* 5 (1967), pp. 896-904.

—'Zu Phil II 7: EKENΩΣEN EAΥTON', *NovT* 6 (1963), pp. 182-88.

Johnson, L.T., 'Romans 3.21-26 and the Faith of Jesus', *CBQ* 44 (1982), pp. 77-90.

de Jonge, H.J., 'The earliest traceable stage of the textual tradition of the Testaments of the Twelve Patriarchs', *Studies on the Testaments of the Twelve Patriarchs*, edited by M. de Jonge (SVTP, 3; Leiden: Brill, 1975), pp. 63-86.

—'Die Textüberlieferung der Testamente der zwölf Patriarchen', *Studies on the Testaments of the Twelve Patriarchs*, edited by M. de Jonge (SVTP, 3; Leiden: Brill, 1975), pp. 45-62.

—'Christian Influence in the Testaments of the Twelve Patriarchs', *Studies on the Testaments of the Twelve Patriarchs*, edited by M. de Jonge (SVTP 3; Leiden: Brill, 1975), pp. 193-246.

—*Testamenta XII Patriarchum* (Pseudepigrapha Veteris Testamenti Graece, 1; Leiden: Brill, 1964).

—*The Testaments of the Twelve Patriarchs* (Van Gorcums Theologische Bibliothek, 25; 2nd edn; Assen & Amsterdam: Van Gorcum, 1975).

Juel, D., 'The Image of the Servant-Christ in the New Testament', *SWJT* 21 (1979), pp. 7-22.

Käsemann, E., *Commentary on Romans*, translated and edited by G.W. Bromiley (Grand Rapids: Eerdmans, 1980).

—'Critical Analysis of Philippians 2.5-11', translated by A.F. Carse, edited by R.W. Funk, *Journal for Theology and the Church* 5 (1968), pp. 45-88.

—'The Pauline Doctrine of the Lord's Supper', *Essays on New Testament Themes*, translated by W.J. Montague (SBT, 41; Naperville, Illinois: Allenson 1964), pp. 108-25.

—'The Saving Significance of Jesus' Death in Paul', *Perspectives on Paul*, translated by M. Kohl (Philadelphia: Fortress, 1971), pp. 32-59.

—'Zum Verständnis von Römer 3, 24-26', *ZNW* 43 (1950-51), pp. 150-54

Kane, J.P., 'The Mithraic cult meal in its Greek and Roman environment', *Mithraic Studies* II, edited by J.R. Hinnells (Manchester: Manchester University Press, 1975), pp. 313-51.

Kee, H.C., 'Testaments of the Twelve Patriarchs', *The Old Testament Pseudepigrapha*, 2 volumes, edited by J.H. Charlesworth (Garden City, New York: Doubleday, 1983), Vol. I, pp. 775-828.

Kennedy, H.A.A., *St. Paul and the Mystery Religions* (London: Holder & Stoughton, 1913).

Kennett, R.H., *The Last Supper* (Cambridge: Heffers, 1921).

Kertelge, K., 'Exegetische Überlegungen zum Verständnis der paulinischen Anthropologie nach Römer 7', *ZNW* 62 (1971), pp. 105-14.

—*'Rechtfertigung' bei Paulus* (NA, 3, new series; Münster: Aschendorff, 1967).

Klappert, B., 'Zur Frage des semitischen oder griechischen Urtextes von 1 Kor. XV.3-5', *NTS* 13 (1966-67), pp. 168-73.

Klauck, H.-J., *Herrenmahl und hellenistischer Kult* (Neutestamentliche Abhandlungen, new series 15; Münster: Aschendorff, 1982).

—*1 Korintherbrief* (NEcB, 7; Würzburg: Echter, 1984).

Klein, G., *Studien über Paulus* (Stockholm: Bonniers, 1918).

Kloppenborg, J., 'An Analysis of the Pre-Pauline Formula 1 Cor 15.3b-5 in Light of Some Recent Literature', *CBQ* 40 (1978), pp. 351-67.

Knox, W.L., *Some Hellenistic Elements in Primitive Christianity* (London: British Academy [H. Milford], 1944).

Kortweg, T., 'Further observation of the transmission of the text', *Studies on the Testaments of the Twelve Patriarchs*, edited by M. de Jonge (SVTP, 3; Leiden: Brill, 1975), pp. 161-73.

Kramer, W., *Christ, Lord, Son of God* (SBT, 50; Naperville, Illinois: Allenson, 1966).

Kremer, J., *Das älteste Zeugnis von der Auferstehung Christi* (SB, 17; Stuttgart: Verlag Katholisches Bibelwerk, 1967).

Krinetzki, L., *Das Einfluss von der Is LII, 13-LIII, 12 Par. auf Phil. II.6-11* (Rome: Pontificum Athenaeum Anselmianum, 1959).

Kümmel, W.G., *Römer 7 und die Bekehrung des Paulus* (Leipzig: Hinrichs'sche Buchhandlung, 1929).

Kuss, O., *Der Römerbrief*, 3 volumes (Regensburg: Pustet, 1963-78).

—'Die theologischen Grundgedanken des Hebräerbriefes. Zur Deutung des Todes Jesu im Neuen Testament', *Auslegung und Verkündigung*, 3 volumes (Regensburg: Pustet, 1963), pp. 281-328.

Larson, E., *Christus als Vorbild* (Acta seminarii Neotestamentici Upsaliensis, 23; Lund: Gleerup, 1962).

Le Déaut, R., *La Nuit Pascale* (AnBib, 22; Rome: Institut Biblique Pontifical, 1963).

Lehmann, K., *Auferweckt am dritten Tag nach der Schrift* (QD, 38; Freiburg, Basel & Vienna: Herder, 1968).

Lietzmann, H., *An die Korinther I-II* (HNT, 9; edited by W.G. Kümmel; 4th edn, Tübingen: Mohr [Paul Siebeck], 1949).

—*An die Römer* (HNT, 8; 5th edn; Tübingen: Mohr [Siebeck], 1971).

—*Mass and Lord's Supper*, translated by D.H.G. Reeve (Leiden: Brill, 1979).

Lohse, B., *Das Passafest der Quartadecimaner* (BFChTh, 2nd Series, 54; Gütersloh: Bertelsmann, 1953).

—*Märtyrer und Gottesknecht* (Göttingen: Vandenhoeck & Ruprecht, 1955).

—*The New Testament Environment* translated by J.E. Steely (Nashville: Abingdon, 1976).

Loisy, Alfred F., *The Birth of the Christian Religion*, translated by L.P. Jacks (New Hyde Park, New York: University Books, 1962).

Lövestam, E., *Spiritual Wakefulness in the New Testament* (Lunds Universitets Arsskrift, N.F. Avd. 1., Vol. 55, No. 3; Lund: Gleerup, 1963).

Lucian, *Lucian*, translated by A.M. Harmon, K. Kilburn, and M.D. Macleod (LCL; London: Heinemann; Cambridge, Massachusetts: Harvard University Press; New York: Macmillan; New York: Putman, 1913-67).

Lucian, 'Demonax', *The Works of Lucian*, translated by A.M. Harmon (LCL; Cambridge, Massachusetts: Harvard University Press; London: William Heinemann Ltd., 1961).

Lyonnet, S., 'Péché', *Dictionnaire de la bible. Supplément*, edited by L. Pirot *et al.* (Paris: Letouzey & Ané, 1966), pp. 407-567.

—and Sabourin, L., *Sin, Redemption, and Sacrifice* (AnBib, 48; Rome: Biblical Institute Press, 1970).

McGinty, P., *Interpretation and Dionysos* (RR, 16; The Hague, Paris & New York: Morton, 1978).

Machen, J.G., *The Origin of Paul's Religion* (New York: Macmillan, 1921).

MacMullen, R., *Paganism in the Roman Empire* (New Haven and London: Yale University Press, 1981).

Malherbe, A.J., 'Antisthenes and Odysseus, and Paul at War', *HTR* 76 (1983), pp. 143-74.

Manson, T.W., 'ΙΛΑΣΤΗΡΙΟΝ', *JTS* 46 (1945), pp. 1-10.

—'Romans', *Peake's Commentary*, edited by M. Black (New York: Nelson, 1962), pp. 940-53.

Marcellinus, Ammianus, *Ammianus Marcellinus*, translated by J.C. Rolfe (LCL; Cambridge, Massachusetts: Harvard University Press; London: William Heinemann, 1935-39).

Martin, R.P., *Carmen Christi* (SNTSMS, 4; Cambridge: Cambridge University Press, 1967).

Metzger, B.M. 'Methodology in the Study of the Mystery Religions and Early Christianity', *Historical and Literary Studies* (NTTS, 8; Grand Rapids, Michigan: Eerdmans, 1968), pp. 1-24.

Michaelis, W., *Der Brief des Paulus an die Philipper* (ThHK, II; Leipzig: Deichert, 1935).

Michel, O., *Der Brief an die Römer* (KEK, 4; 5th edn; Göttingen: Vandenhoeck & Ruprecht, 1978).

—'Zur Exegese von Phil 2.5-11', *Theologie als Glaubenswagnis* (Hamburg: Furche-Verlag, 1954), pp. 79-95.

Minde, H.-J. van der, *Schrift und Tradition bei Paulus* (PTS, 3; Munich, Paderborn & Vienna: Schöningh, 1976).

Morgan, F.A., 'Romans 6,5a: United to a Death like Christ's', *ETL* 59 (1983), pp. 267-302.

Morris, L., *The Apostolic Preaching of the Cross*, 3rd edn (Grand Rapids: Eerdmans, 1965).

—'The Meanings of ἱλάσκεσθαι in Romans iii.25', *NTS* 2, (1955), pp. 33-43.

Moulton, J.H., *A Grammar of the Greek New Testament*, 3 volumes (Edinburgh: Clark, 1906-63).

Murphy-O'Connor, J., 'Tradition and Redaction in 1 Cor. 15.3-7', *CBQ* 43 (1981), pp. 582-89.

Mussner, F., *Der Galaterbrief* (HThK, 9; Freiburg, Basel & Vienna: Herder, 1974).

Nash, R.H., *Christianity and the Hellenistic World* (Grand Rapids, Michigan: Zondervan; Dallas: Probe Ministries International, 1984).

Neuenzeit, P., *Das Herrenmahl* (StANT, 1; Munich: Kösel, 1960).

Nickelsburg, G.W.E., *Jewish Literature between the Bible and Mishnah* (Philadelphia: Fortress, 1981).

Nilsson, M.P., 'The Bacchic Mysteries of the Roman Age', *HTR* 46 (1953), pp. 175-202.

—*The Dionysiac Mysteries of the Hellenistic and Roman Age* (Skrifter Utgivna av Svenska Institutet i Athen 8; Lund: Gleerup, 1957).

—*Geschichte des griechischen Religion*, 2nd edn, 2 volumes (Munich: Beck, 1955-57).

Nock, A.D., *Conversion* (Oxford: Clarendon, 1933).

—'Early Gentile Christianity and its Hellenistic Background', *Essays on Religion and the Ancient World*, edited by Z. Stewart, 2 volumes (Cambridge, Massachusetts: Harvard University Press, 1972), Vol. I, pp. 49-133.

—'Eunuchs in Ancient Religion', *Essays on Religion and the Ancient World*, 2 volumes, edited by Z. Stewart (Cambridge, Massachusetts: Harvard University Press, 1972), Vol. I, pp. 7-15.

—'Hellenistic Mysteries and Christian Sacraments', *Essays on Religion and the Ancient World*, 2 volumes, edited by Z. Stewart (Cambridge, Massachusetts: Harvard University Press, 1972), Vol. II, pp. 791-820.

Norden, E., *Die Antike Kunstprosa*, 5th edn, Vol. I (Darmstadt: Wissenschaftliche Buchgesellschaft, 1958).

Nygren, A., *Commentary on Romans* (Philadelphia: Muhlenburg, 1949).

Oepke, A., *Der Brief des Paulus an die Galater*, edited by J. Rohde (ThHK, 9; Berlin: Evangelische Verlagsanstalt, 1973).

—'ἐν', *TDNT* 2 (1964), pp. 537-43.

—'παῖς', *TDNT* 5 (1967), pp. 636-54.

Orr, W.F. and Walther, J.A., *I Corinthians* (AB, 32; Garden City, Doubleday, 1976).

Osten-Sacken, P. von der, *Römer 8 als Beispiel paulinischer Soteriologie* (Göttingen: Vandenhoeck & Ruprecht, 1975).

Ovid, *Metamorphoses*, translated by F.J. Miller (LCL; Cambridge, Massachusetts: Harvard University Press; London: Heinemann, 1958-60.

Page, S.H.T., 'The Suffering Servant Between the Testaments', *NTS* 31 (1985), pp. 481-97.

Patsch, H., 'Zum alttestamentlichen Hintergrund von Römer 4.25 und I. Petrus 2.24', *ZNW* 60 (1969), pp. 273-79.

Paulsen, H., *Überlieferung und Auslegung in Römer 8* (WMANT, 43; Neukirchen-Vluyn: Neukirchener Verlag, 1974).

Perkins, P., *Reading the New Testament* (New York & Ramsey, New Jersey: Paulist Press, 1978).

Perrin, N., 'The Use of (παρα)διδόναι in Connection with the Passion of Jesus in the New Testament', *Der Ruf Jesu und die Antwort der Gemeinde*, edited by E. Lohse with C. Burchard and B. Schaller (Göttingen: Vandenhoeck & Ruprecht, 1970), pp. 204-12.

Pesch, R., *Das Abendmahl und Jesu Todverständnis* (QD, 80; Freiburg, Basel & Vienna: Herder, 1978).

—*Römerbrief* (NEcB, 6; Würzburg: Echter Verlag, 1983).

Peterson, E., *Frühkirche, Judentum und Gnosis* (Rome, Freiburg & Vienna: Herder, 1959).

Pfitzner, V.C., *Paul and the Agon Motif* (SNT, 16; Leiden: Brill, 1967).

Pluta, A., *Gottes Bundestreue* (SBS, 34; Stuttgart: Verlag Katholisches Bibelwerk, 1969).

Plutarch, *Lives*, translated by B. Perrin (LCL; London: Heinemann; New York: Macmillan; New York: Putnam, 1914-26).

—*Moralia*, 14 volumes translated by F.C. Babbit, P.A. Clement, H.B. Hoffleit, E.L. Minar, Jr, F.H. Sandbach, W.C. Helmbold, H.N. Fowler, L. Pearson, H. Cherness, B. Einarson, and P.H. De Lacy (LCL; New York: Putnam; Cambridge, Massachusetts: Harvard University Press; London: Heinemann, 1927-69).

Pobee, J.S., *Persecution and Martyrdom in the Theology of Paul* (JSNTS, 6; Sheffield, England: JSOT Press, 1985).

Popkes, W., *Christus Traditus* (AThANT, 49; Zürich & Stuttgart: Zwingli, 1967).

Rahner, H., 'Das christliche Mysterium und die heidnischen Mysterien', *Eranos Jahrbuch*, edited by O. Frobe-Kapteyn, II (1944), pp. 347-98.

Reicke, B., 'Der Gottesknecht im Alten und Neuen Testament', *ThZ* 35 (1979), pp. 342-50.

Renehan, R., 'The Greek Philosophic Background of Fourth Maccabees', *Rheinisches Museum für Philologie* 115, 1972.

Rese, M., 'Überprüfung einiger Thesen von Joachim Jeremias zum Thema des Gottesknechtes im Judentum', *ZTK* 60 (1963), pp. 21-41.

Reventlow, H. von., *Opfere deinen Sohn* (BS, 53; Neukirchen-Vluyn: Neukirchener Verlag, 1968).

Richardson, N.J., 'Early Greek views about life after death', *Greek Religion and Society*, edited by P.E. Easterling and J.V. Muir (Cambridge: Cambridge University Press, 1985), pp. 50-66.

Robertson, N., 'The Ritual of the Dying God in Cyprus and Syro-Palestine', *HTR* 75 (1982), pp. 313-60.

Romaniuk, K., 'L'Origine des formules pauliniennes "Le Christ s'est livré pour nous", "Le Christ nous a aimés et s'est livré pour nous" ', *NovT* 5 (1962), pp. 55-76.

Sanders, E.P., *Paul and Palestinian Judaism* (Philadelphia: Fortress, 1977).

Sasse, H., 'αἰών.', *TDNT* 1 (1963), pp. 197-209.

Schade, H.-H., *Apokalyptische Christologie bei Paulus* (GTA, 18; Göttingen: Vandenhoeck & Ruprecht, 1981).

Schelkle, K.H., *Die Passion Jesu in der Verkündigung des Neuen Testaments* (Heidelberg: Kerle, 1949).

Schlier, H., *Der Brief an die Galater* (KEK, 7; 14th edn; Göttingen: Vandenhoeck & Ruprecht, 1971).

—*Der Römerbrief* (HThK, 6; Freiburg, Basel & Vienna: Herder, 1977).

Schmidt, H.W., *Der Brief des Paulus an die Römer* (ThHK, 6; Berlin: Evangelische Verlagsanstalt, 1962).

Schnackenburg, R., *Baptism in the thought of St. Paul*, translated by G.R. Beasley-Murray (Oxford: Blackwell, 1964).

—'Christologie des Neuen Testaments', in *Das Christusereignis*. Volume III; Part 1 of *Mysterium Salutis. Grundriss heilsgeschichtlicher Dogmatik*, edited by J. Feiner and M. Löhrer (Einsiedeln, Zurich & Cologne: Benziger, 1970), pp. 227-388.

Schnelle, U., *Gerechtigkeit und Christusgegenwart* (Göttingen: Vandenhoeck & Ruprecht, 1973).

Schoeps, H.J., *Paul: The Theology of the Apostle in the Light of Jewish Religious History*, translated by Harold Knight (Philadelphia: Westminster, 1961).

—'The Sacrifice of Isaac in Paul's Theology', *JBL* 65 (1946), pp. 385-92.

Schrenk, G., 'βιάζομαι', *TDNT* 1 (1964), pp. 609-14.

Schürmann, E., *Der Einsetzungsbericht* (NA, 20; Münster: Aschendorff, 1955).

Schweitzer, A., *The Mysticism of Paul the Apostle*, translated by W. Montgomery (London: Black, 1931).

Schweizer, E., 'Dying and Rising with Christ', *NTS* 14 (1967), pp. 1-14.

—'Die hellenistischen Komponente im neutestamentlichen σάρξ-Begriff', *ZNW* 48 (1957), pp. 237-53.

—*The Lord's Supper according to the New Testament*, translated by J.M. Davis (Philadelphia: Fortress, 1967).

—*Lordship and Discipleship* (SBT, 28; Naperville, Illinois: Allenson, 1960).

Seeberg, A., *Der Katechismus der Urchristenheit* (Leipzig: Deichert, 1903).

Seneca, *Ad Luculium Epistulae Morales*, 3 volumes, translated by R.M. Gummere (LCL; Cambridge, Massachusetts: Harvard University Press; London: Heinemann, 1947).

—'De Providentia', *Moral Essays*, translated by J.W. Basore (LCL; London: Heinemann; New York: Putman, 1928).

Showerman, G., *The Great Mother of the Gods* (Madison, Wisconsin: University of Wisconsin Press, 1901).

Silius Italicus, *Punica*, 2 volumes, translated by J.D. Duff (LCL; Cambridge, Massachusetts: Harvard University Press; London: Heinemann, 1949).

Simon, M., 'The *Religionsgeschichtliche Schule*, Fifty Years Later', *Religious Studies* 2 (1975). pp. 135-44.

Slingerland, H.D., *The Testaments of the Twelve Patriarchs: A Critical History of Research* (SBLDS, 21; Missoula, Montana: Scholars Press, 1975).

Smith, M., 'On the Problem of Method in the Study of Rabbininc Literature', *JBL* 92 (1973), pp. 112-13.

—*Palestinian Parties and Politics that Shaped the Old Testament World* (Lectures on the history of religions, new series 9; New York: Columbia University Press, 1971).

Stählin, G., Ἴσος *TDNT* 3 (1965).

Stambaugh, J.E., *Sarapis under the Early Ptolemies* (EPRO, 25; Leiden: Brill, 1972).

Stanley, D.M., *Christ's Resurrection in Pauline Soteriology* (AnBib, 13; Rome: Pontifical Biblical Institute, 1961).

—'The Theme of the Servant of Yahweh in Primitive Christian Soteriology and its Transposition by St. Paul', *CBQ* 16 (1954), pp. 385-425.

Strecker, G., 'Befreiung und Rechtfertigung. Zur Stellung der Rechtfertigungslehre in der Theologie des Paulus', *Rechtfertigung*, edited by J. Friedrich, W. Pöhlmann and P. Stuhlmacher (Tübingen: Mohr [Paul Siebeck]; Göttingen: Vandenhoeck & Ruprecht, 1976), pp. 479-508.

—'Redaktion und Tradition im Christushymnus Phil 2.6-11', *ZNW* 55 (1964), pp. 63-78.

Stuhlmacher, P., 'Theologische Probleme gegenwärtiger Paulusinterpretation', *TLZ* 98 (1973), pp. 721-32.

—'Zur neueren Exegese von Röm 3.24-26', *Jesus und Paulus*, edited by E.E. Ellis and E. Grässer (Göttingen: Vandenhoeck & Ruprecht, 1975), pp. 315-33.

Surkau, H.-W., *Märtyrien in jüdischer und früh-christlicher Zeit* (FRLANT, 54; Göttingen: Vandenhoeck & Ruprecht, 1938).

Swetnam, J., *Jesus and Isaac* (AnBib, 94; Rome: Biblical Institute Press, 1981).

Tacitus, *The Annals*, translated by J. Jackson (LCL; Cambridge, Massachusetts: Harvard University Press; London: Heinemann, 1951).

Talbert, C.H. 'The Problem of Pre-Existence in Phil. 2.6-1', *JBL* 86 (1967), pp. 141-53.

Theocritus, *The Idylls of Theocritus*, translated by T. Sargent (New York and London: Norton, 1982).

Torrey, C.C., *The Apocryphal Literature* (New Haven: Yale University, 1945).

Townshend, R.B., '4 Maccabees', *The Apocrypha and Pseudepigrapha of the Old Testament*, 2 volumes, edited by R.H. Charles (Oxford: Clarendon, 1913), vol. II, pp. 653-85.

Turner, N., *Syntax* (Edinburgh: Clark, 1963).

Vermes, G., 'Redemption and Genesis xxii—The Binding of Isaac and the Sacrifice of Jesus', *Scripture and Tradition in Judaism* (SPB, 4; 2nd edn; Leiden: Brill, 1973), pp. 193-227.

Vidman, L., *Isis und Sarapis bei den Griechen und Römern* (Berlin: de Gruyter, 1970).

Wacholder, B.Z., 'The Date of the Mekilta de-Rabbi Ishmael', *HUCA* 39 (1968), pp. 117-44.

—'A Reply', *JBL* 92 (1973), pp. 114-15.

—Review of M. McNamara, *Targum and Testament, JBL* 93 (1974), pp. 132-33.

Wagner, G., *Pauline Baptism and the Pagan Mysteries*, translated by J.P. Smith (Edinburgh & London: Oliver & Boyd, 1967).

Wedderburn, A.J.M., 'Hellenistic Christian Traditions in Romans 6?' *NTS* 29, pp. 337-55.

—'The Soteriology of the Mysteries and Pauline Baptismal Theology', *NovT* 29 (1987), pp. 53-72.

Weiss, B., *Kritisch-exegetisches Handbuch über den Brief des Paulus an die Römer* (7th edn Göttingen: Vandenhoeck & Ruprecht, 1886).

Weiss, J., *Der erste Korintherbrief* (KEK, 5; 10th edn; Göttingen: Vandenhoeck & Ruprecht, 1925).

Wengst, K., *Christologische Formeln und Lieder des Urchristentums* (Gütersloh: Mohn, 1972).

Wiens, D.H., 'Mystery Concepts in Primitive Christianity and its Environment', *ANRW* II/23.2 (1980), pp. 1248-84.

Wilckens, U., *Der Brief an die Römer* (EKK, 6; Zürich: Benziger; Neukirchen-Vluyn: Neukirchener Verlag, 1978-82)

Wilcox, M., ' "Upon the Tree"—Deut. 21.22-23 in the New Testament', *JBL* 96 (1977), pp. 85-99.

Williams, S.K., *Jesus' Death as Saving Event: The Origin of a Concept* (HDR, 2; Missoula, Montana: Scholars Press, 1975).

—'The "Righteousness of God" in Romans', *JBL* 99 (1980), pp. 241-90.

Willis, W.L., *Idol Meat in Corinth* (SBLDS, 68; Chico, California: Scholars Press, 1985).

Wilson, T., *St. Paul and Paganism* (Edinburgh: Clark, 1927).

Wolff, C., *Der erste Brief des Paulus an die Korinther* (ThHK, 7; Part 2; Berlin: Evangelische Verlagsanstalt, 1982).

Wood, L.E., 'Isaac Typology in the New Testament', *NTS* 14 (1967-68), pp. 583-89.

Young, N.H., ' "Hilaskesthai" and Related Words in the New Testament', *EvQ* 55 (1983), pp. 169-76.

Zeitlin, S., *The Second Book of Maccabees*, edited by S. Zeitlin, translated by S. Tedesche (New York: Published for the Dropsie College for Hebrew and Cognate Learning by Harper & Brothers, 1954).

INDEXES

INDEX OF BIBLICAL REFERENCES

HEBREW BIBLE

NEW TESTAMENT

INDEX OF AUTHORS